STOP HIDING:

Unlock Your Full Potential and Embrace the 5

Pillars of a Growth Mindset

JOCELYN M. LEE, DM

Unless otherwise noted Scripture passages are taken from the English Standard Version, New Living Translation, New International Translation, and/or the author's own translation.

Website: msjocelynlee.com

To contact Jocelyn Nolan Lee for speaking arrangements, please email info@jocelynmlee.com.

ISBN: 979-8-218-23321-1

Cover design: Rica Graphics

Interior design: fiverr/MalikAhsan396

Photography: Dana Gibbons

To Ethel

Mother, you are the genesis of this beautiful path that I tread.

TABLE OF CONTENTS

Divine Espresso

Yes, I'll take a Venti Belief, please, with an extra shot of Self-Insight. And could I have the Intellect and Ability sandwich, please? For dessert, a serving of Spirit. I'll enjoy it here because I live in the moment.

–JOCELYN

INTRODUCTION

Disponibilité

"Remain available" to the things themselves; the fresh voice, the one that sounds the strangest, your unalienated voice; for it does not sound like your habitual voice, and in a weird sort of way it is your real voice, the call to authenticity.

-The Phenomenology of Edmund Husserl

In the arid valleys of Phoenix, Arizona where the implacable sun reigns supreme for most of the year, there exists a seasonal phenomenon that dramatically alters the landscape and realities of its residents. Monsoon season, an annual spectacle descends upon the city like a tempestuous guest, unwelcome yet unavoidable.

As the sweltering summer grips the city, the anticipation of nature's fury looms in the air. With its ominous warning signs of darkening skies and distant rumbles, the Monsoon ushers in a torrent of chaos. Rain, a rare visitor in the region falls in relentless sheets, transforming parched earth into muddy torrents. Lightning dances across the heavens, illuminating the desert like a celestial firework show, while thunder booms like a primal drum beat. The wind once a gentle sight, becomes a ferocious force, whipping through palm fronds and sending debris hurtling through the air.

One such tumultuous night, just before retiring, my husband and I were alerted by Solomon, our loyal Labrador, barking and panting in front of the patio door. Because it was very dark outside, we couldn't see what had gotten his attention, but we could tell he was exasperated. Solomon had sensed disruptive activity in the shadows and alerted us to come and take notice. I walked to the door and flicked on the patio light to see what he saw in the darkness. The patio illuminated, I could see the wind whipping through the foliage, loose debris flying through the air, and wicker furniture spinning violently.

The moment was revelatory. Provoked by the chaos and disruption emerging from the shadows, I was inspired to emerge from the shadows in my own life to share my journey and the lessons therein. I am reminded of the Scripture, "But all things become visible when they are exposed by the light, for everything that becomes visible is light" (Ephesians 5:13).

I have come across countless women who desire more from life and in themselves. I know them; I am them, and I am dedicated to encouraging women on their journeys to self-actualization. These lessons are not theories but lived experiences. I know a thing or two about hiding and later stepping out.

As a girl, I hid behind jazz and tap dance when my ballet teacher, unimpressed with the elevation of my grand jetés told me—perhaps trying to appear sympathetic—that my butt was a handicap, and I'd never make it as a ballerina. "You should try something else," she said. Her words fractured parts of me. I became convinced that ballet wasn't for black girls with big butts, and my body type did not fit the ballet aesthetic. At that time, my belief seemed set in stone, and I saw no way to change it. I had given up my dreams of becoming a ballerina by the time the incredibly talented Misty Copeland appeared on the scene breaking down barriers and stereotypes to jeté over obstacles and doubters.

In my teen years, I hid behind the nickname, "Chub," bestowed upon me by endearing relatives. I associated this term with being overweight and compared myself to my cousins, who were thinner than me. Chubby was what I would become. I grew into that person and made excuses for my weight. Thinking it was a negative trait, I resigned myself to being *big-boned*, something I could not change mind you, but a characteristic I have now come to embrace.

When my mother and I moved from my birthplace Dayton, Ohio to Milwaukee, we briefly lived with a large family until Mom found us a place of our own. The matriarch of the family was very gracious; however, looking back, I realized dinner time was often stressful. There were a lot of mouths to feed, and often I left the dinner table hungry. After returning from work later in the evening, my mother would sneak me into the kitchen, hide me between an appliance and the kitchen table, and sneak me food.

When I recently asked my mother why she did this, she couldn't recall the specific reason but felt it was 'something she needed to do.' While her actions were likely driven by maternal instincts, they inadvertently led to a pattern of unhealthy eating habits. I didn't notice until much later in life that I preferred eating alone.

Throughout my career, I often traveled with colleagues who enjoyed coming together for a working lunch or dinner. Some of the gatherings I could not escape; however, when I managed to get away with it, I would make excuses. I'd have a meeting or conference call I simply *had* to attend, or work I needed to catch up on in my hotel room. I would often retreat there, so I could be alone with my food.

While I love to go out on a dinner date with my husband or with friends, I still prefer take-out. Without delving into the psychological nuances, I'll simply say that I've spent more time eating alone than with others. Thank God, I now have the tools to help me overcome unhealthy eating habits!

But my early years of hiding didn't stop there. At times, it was necessary to accompany my mom to work because she couldn't trust someone else to look after me. While she worked, I hid, literally, under her desk. Nestled beneath her desk, my quest for invisibility evolved into a childhood adventure. Little did I know how this inclination would manifest in my adult life, often in unfavorable ways: I allowed people in corporate America to render me invisible by devaluing my contributions. I would simply put my head down, work hard, and hide at my desk, shrouded in my insecurities behind less talented and capable people. Caught in a cycle of self-doubt, I often found myself hiding behind my academic achievements as if my degrees could validate my worth.

Realizing that I had more to offer than what I was putting into the world, I embarked on a journey of self-discovery. I knew I could not continue to hide in the shadows behind someone else's expectations and my own feelings of inadequacy. I hid behind a persona and sought comfort in the shadows. Chaos and distraction invaded my life much in the same way an unexpected late-night Monsoon episode would capture my attention many years later.

From hiding behind nicknames and ballet stereotypes to sneaking extra meals and ducking under desks, I've spent a significant portion of my life in the shadows literally and metaphorically. It is from these lived experiences that the idea of *Stop Hiding* was born. My goal is to share the knowledge and teachings that I have come to possess over time. In areas where my personal experiences did not suffice, I sought insight from other writers, researchers, and thinkers to bring diverse perspectives and depth to the book.

***

Discovery of a Different Kind

A pivotal moment came during a gathering to celebrate my doctorate degree. A friend asked me a question that has lingered in my thoughts to this day. "What did you learn?" he asked. To which I responded, "I learned how much I don't know." This realization serves as a constant reminder that the journey of learning is never-ending, regardless of how much knowledge one accumulates. Eventually, I realized that true wisdom extends far beyond academic accolades.

I am devoted to learning new things. Some of this knowledge has been acquired through intellectual pursuits, while others have been imparted to me by teachers worldwide. However, most of my wisdom has come from participation as a perpetual student, constantly seeking new experiences and insights. This perpetual quest for knowledge and insight has been my way of stepping out of the shadows, embracing complexities, and owning my story.

***

The Superwoman Persona

Born to two incredible individuals whose world as a married couple was too small to manifest their hopes and dreams together, I navigated a complex family landscape from a young age. My parents' separation and eventual divorce shaped my character in profound ways. Raised by a resilient mother and a supportive community, I grew into an ambitious extroverted individual with a knack for survival.

While my father was a source of affirmation when present, his intermittent absences left a gap that contributed to feelings of low self-esteem. This emotional void fueled my drive to overachieve yet left me grappling with a sense of never quite being good enough. For years, I chased success as defined by societal norms-climbing the corporate ladder, accumulating degrees, and striving to be "superwoman." This relentless pursuit often came at the expense of being present for my family and disconnected me from my true self. Nevertheless, life has a way of teaching us what we need to know.

***

An Introduction to Disruptive Thinking

I have chosen not to *hold back* in these compact pages, an admonishment given on more than one occasion from a certain professor who rebuked me for trying to teach *everything* I had learned. These words are my thoughts out loud; and, no matter how hard I try to keep them to myself, I am devoted to sharing. In the words of one of my favorite philosophers Merleau Ponty, "My own words take me by surprise and teach me what to think."

If you are experiencing current chaos, or simply desire something new and different in your life, know that your circumstances contain the disruptive power of potential beckoning you to step out of the shadows and realize a whole new world is waiting for you! My purpose is to help individuals, especially women, embrace a growth mindset to overcome challenges, develop resilience, and unlock their full capabilities.

***

Embracing the Light of Authenticity

Our Creator gives us the potential to fulfill our purpose on earth and experience passion. My desire is for you to use your light to discover who you are and, in turn, pass it on. I've found immense value in embracing God's light, and I feel called to share that light in hopes it might illuminate paths for others.

This book is an invitation to consider that now might be the time for you to step into your own light, rather than keeping it hidden. If you find yourself engaged in an ongoing inner dialogue, it could be a sign that there's untapped potential waiting to be discovered. My hope is that the lessons in this book will offer you insights to bolster your confidence, and inner strength, allowing you not only to find your way but also to light the way for others. Organizational psychologist Adam Grant in his book *Think Again* says it best, "The purpose of learning isn't to affirm our beliefs; it's to evolve our beliefs." May contemplating my words contribute to your growth mindset.

***

Dueling Mindsets

In this book, we embark on a transformative journey challenging you to evolve your beliefs and grow your mindset. As you delve deeper into the depths of these pages, and if you are seeking personal and professional growth, you will encounter a tapestry that weaves together diverse spiritual, philosophical, and experiential wisdom. To summarize Joan of Arc (1412-1431), if "I encounter your truth may God keep me there, if I do not, may God lead me there."

Curating from a variety of sources, most notably, the work of Dr. Carol Dweck in *Mindset: The New Psychology of Success*, I share the Five Pillars of a growth mindset to help individuals on the journey to self-discovery and empowerment. Before I introduce the pillars, however, it is important to discuss the concept of *dueling mindsets*, fixed vs growth.

***

Have you ever found yourself hiding—either metaphorically or literally—because you felt like you couldn't change or improve? If so, you may be operating under a fixed mindset, a perspective that can limit your potential and keep you in the shadows. Hiding often signals the presence of a fixed mindset, a viewpoint that sees personal attributes as unchangeable. This mindset convinces you that your abilities, intelligence, and qualities are static, leaving no room for growth or development. This mindset often leads people to risk avoidance and a reluctance to step out of their comfort zones, driven by the fear that failure could tarnish their self-image. Such individuals may also hesitate to tackle challenges that demand sustained effort, convinced that no amount of practice can enhance their innate ability.

In this book, we'll explore how a fixed mindset, contrasts with a growth mindset, which opens the door to evolution and self-improvement. A fixed perspective can trap you in a cycle of constantly trying to validate your worth, as you operate under the assumption that you're limited to a set amount of intelligence or talent. In essence, those with a fixed mindset view their capabilities as pre-determined, interpreting challenges and setbacks as reflections of their limitation rather than as opportunities for growth.

I can attest from personal experience that living with a fixed mindset can be a draining quest for external validation, one that hampers your ability to recognize your own worth. If you find yourself in this mindset, know that it can keep you from reaching your full potential and fulfilling your true purpose.

On the other hand, embracing a growth mindset can be a game-changer in realizing your untapped potential. Unlike a fixed mindset, which confines you to a limited view of your abilities, and plagues you with fear and doubt, a growth mindset opens up a world of possibilities. It encourages you to see challenges as opportunities for development, regardless of your biological, cultural, or personal background. This mindset empowers you to evolve continuously, fueled by new knowledge and experiences.

Instead of being tethered to innate traits, a growth mindset invites you on a lifelong journey of self-improvement. It serves as a motivational force, inspiring you to take courageous steps and invest the effort needed to achieve your goals.

Ryan Holiday writes in *The Obstacle is the Way*, "When you have a goal, obstacles are actually teaching you how to get where you want to go—carving you a path." And most [obstacles] he says are "internal." Such self-imposed limitations can stifle your potential, leaving you discouraged and less likely to strive for growth.

***

The Five Growth Mindset Pillars

The good news is there's a way to navigate through these barriers. In the chapters that follow, we'll delve into the transformative power of a growth mindset through my Five Pillars: *Belief, Abilities, Self-Insight, Intellect, and Spirit.* Each pillar serves as a stepping stone, guiding you on a journey of self-discovery and empowerment.

Theologian, Joan Chittister, wrote in *An Evolving God, An Evolving Purpose, An Evolving World,* "the call to purpose points us up one idea, then down another until we find the right path." How amazing is that? We get to make something of the light which releases its power when we shine through our potential. We are trusted with the light to better ourselves and leave a trail for others to follow, for this is the goal and life's reward.

You and I are not a complete blueprint. Through a growth mindset, we can collaborate with our Creator constantly. When the prophetical voices spoke, that God knew us before we were born (Jeremiah 1:5), God didn't just know us then, but God knows us now and knows us as we evolve.

I trust the Five Pillars will inspire you to grow in mind, soul, and spirit! They are dynamic and are positively changing how I think, allowing me to fully embrace a growth mindset. By the time you turn the last page of this book, you'll have a clear understanding of what sets a fixed mindset apart from a growth mindset. You'll also discover practical ways to integrate the Five Pillars to unlock your potential. You'll be able to customize this newfound wisdom to fit your unique journey.

To get the most out of your reading experience, I recommend participating in a reflection at the end of each chapter. For a more detailed exploration, check out the appendix at the end of the book. Both will serve as a toolkit for crafting an action plan that's perfectly aligned with your goals and aspirations. When you show up, insight and inspiration will meet you and you *will* shine through your potential.

***

A Note from the Author

While the lessons shared in this book have proven beneficial in my journey and may resonate with your own experiences, it's important to note that they are not intended to replace professional therapy or serve as a substitute for qualified clinical personnel. If you find yourself facing significant personal challenges or require professional guidance, I strongly encourage seeking the expertise of trained therapists, counselors, or medical professionals who can provide you with specialized support and care you may need.

Xoxo

Jocelyn

CHAPTER ONE

PILLAR #1 BELIEF

One life is all we have and we live it as we believe in living it. But to sacrifice what you are and to live without belief, that is a fate more terrible than dying.

-Joan of Arc

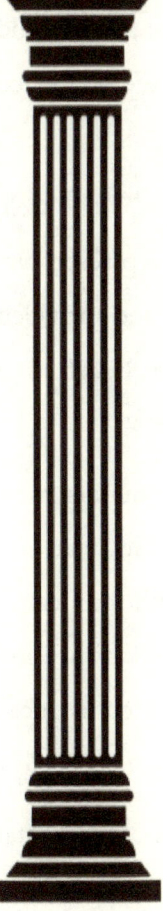

Drawing from the well of belief

In 2010, the world was gripped by the harrowing saga of 32 miners trapped deep underground for 69 days, encased beneath a staggering 700,000 tons of rock in a Chilean mining disaster. The unfolding drama of their rescue efforts captivated global audiences, playing out in real-time on television screens everywhere.

Luis Urzua, the shift foreman worked tirelessly to protect his men and organize their sophisticated underground existence for a month while they endured the most traumatic circumstances. He instructed his men to huddle together to stay warm and leverage resources for safety, while he tasked three miners to accompany him to scout a tunnel. Urzua's leadership was monumental to survival. They rationed food and used heavy equipment to map a tunnel to the latrine. It was further reported that their actions provided the hydration and oxygen needed in order to wait for recovery efforts. They believed in a good outcome. They believed they would be rescued. Their belief fueled their determination, resilience, and collaboration, prompting them to take practical steps to ensure survival.

Al Holland, a psychologist with NASA who rushed to Chile in an effort to share the agency's experience with human isolation said, "I fully believe they will do it [survive]." Holland's remarks highlight the effects of extreme cases of isolation and survival, such as being trapped for long periods of time. The drive to survive can become paramount, leading individuals to tap into their deepest reservoirs of resilience and resourcefulness. This can result in astonishing feats of ingenuity and adaptability as the human spirit fights against the odds. We witnessed such ingenuity in Urzua's actions.

Urzua directing told the other miners, "We need a well." The well, while having a practical application also symbolizes the deep reservoirs of resilience and resourcefulness. His words inspired me and provided me with perspective then and now as I advocate for belief as a foundational pillar of a growth mindset.

I don't have insight into the myriad of emotions the miners went through, I can only make assumptions as to the contradictions, fear, and worry they felt. However, my life has been filled with numerous precarious situations, I can say with certainty that the miners' unwavering belief in their ability to survive and overcome their dire circumstances wasn't just a passive thought but a catalyst for action.

This dynamic connection between belief and action is a fundamental principle of a growth mindset. Just as the miners' beliefs spurred them to seek solutions actively, individuals who embrace a growth mindset are motivated to take intentional steps toward their goals. Believing in their potential empowered the miners to envision success and commit to the hard work, learning, and adaptability required to achieve it. The miners' story is a vivid example of how belief can drive meaningful action, resonating deeply with the spirit of personal growth.

Belief the Cornerstone for a Growth Mindset

To better understand the miners' resolve, we must define what belief looks like. Belief is an option we humans rightfully possess when conclusive evidence for its adequacy is absent; meaning we have the choice to believe in something when there isn't clear and convincing proof that it's true. Belief is like a decision we make when we don't have all the facts.

Applying the philosophical idea of 19th century psychologist, William James, decisions based on hypotheses in causal relationships (if it is this, then it must be that), posit belief as genuine options when the options are living, *meaning of vital concerned*, forced, *because there are no third alternative options*, and momentous, *presenting a unique opportunity of considerable importance*. These relationships support the idea that beliefs are most powerful when they are deeply important to us, when we have to make a choice without any other options, and when that choice could have a big impact on our lives.

The miners' belief in rescue was a choice they made despite not having any guarantee they would be saved. This belief was "living" because it was crucial for survival, "forced" because they had no other options but to believe or give up, and "momentous because their lives literally depended on it. They didn't need logic to believe; the situation itself made belief the most genuine option.

In this harrowing tale of survival, the foreman's call to dig a well was a pivotal moment in laying the groundwork for their collective resilience. The map to the tunnel was their lifeblood, just as digging a well requires going deep enough to penetrate the permeable rock containing water. This act of digging a well serves as a powerful metaphor for the role of belief as the cornerstone of a growth mindset.

***

As I embarked on my own transformational journey, I began to think deeper and more seriously about what I wanted in my life, subordinate to knowing God and making God known. What aspirations lay within the wellspring of grace that cradled my beliefs? What expectations were at the core of my belief?

I was surprised at how fast the answers emerged, and I was pleased with the sharpness and clarity I gained since adopting the Five Pillars of a growth mindset. The first prompting that entered my mind was the **desire to desire** what God desires for me. It has become apparent that God desires me for God's sake, for God's benefit, and for His ambassadorship. God creates desires in me because I have important things to do, and I rely on God's grace to carry out my earthly assignments.

Next, I set the intention to awaken every day with the expectation of drawing from the **well of grace** that encapsulates my beliefs. I envision not only the prospect of worthy achievements but also an unshakable faith that guides me through challenges, nurtures my creations, and cultivates a life of purpose.

Therefore, the metaphoric well demonstrates immense capacity, boundless possibilities, a purposeful path, untapped potential, and profound serenity. Much like the well served as a life-sustaining source for the Chilean miners, belief acts as the foundational wellspring from which the other pillars– self-insight, spirit, intellect, and abilities – draw their sustenance. It's the well of belief that equips individuals to navigate life's challenges and unlock their true potential.

The Power of Belief

The miners' plight wasn't just a story of physical endurance; it was a testament to the power of belief. They had to actively engage with their belief system to survive, much like summoning water from a well when you're parched. Drawing from the well-spring of belief reveals a wealth of transformative elements. As we reach into this well, we will draw from the nourishing waters of self-assurance and resilience.

Submerged in the waters and waiting to be poured out is the confidence to embrace new challenges, the courage to step outside your comfort zone, and the conviction to overcome self-doubt. This well holds the potential to replenish our spirit, offering a deep sense of purpose. The well also symbolizes that there is something to draw from; it's like reaching into the depths of ancient wisdom. We lower the bucket-our vessel of curiosity-down into the abyss-guided by the rope of intention.

As it descends, it passes through layers of time and memory, until it finally kisses the surface of the water-nature's elixir of life. With a gentle tug, we begin the ascent, each rotation of the crank symbolizing the effort it takes to bring hidden treasures to light. And when the bucket emerges, brimming with liquid gold, we realize we've not just drawn water; we have tapped into a reservoir of life's simplest yet most profound miracles to lead us where we want to go.

Belief has the power to shape our attitudes, dictate our behaviors, and ignite our actions, all of which are indispensable components of a growth mindset. When we wholeheartedly trust in our capacity to learn and evolve, we naturally adopt a positive outlook and confront challenges with resilience and determination.

Just as the miners drew upon their deep-seated beliefs to sustain them through unimaginable hardship, so too can we summon our beliefs as a source of strength and direction in our personal and professional lives. Our belief must be strong enough to trust that whatever we believe will come to pass. It's not a magic potion, but it works if you work it.

Think about it this way. When we firmly believe in our ability to accomplish something, we become seekers of opportunities and persist in the face of even the most daunting obstacles, just like Urzua and the trapped miners. Belief is the fuel that propels our motivation, bolsters our determination, and fortifies our resilience, thereby enabling us to achieve the remarkable heights we set out to conquer.

Summoning Your Belief

The power of belief lies within us, often lying dormant until provoked.

This concept of summoning belief resonates deeply with the teachings of Jesus Christ, who frequently posed thought-provoking questions to his followers. Jesus challenged his followers to awaken their own 'living,' 'forced,' and 'momentous' beliefs, pushing them to confront their inner truths and make choices that could profoundly impact their spiritual journey.

He asked:

1. "But who do you say I am?" (Matthew 16:15). Jesus asked this question to his disciples to encourage them to reflect on their understanding of his identity and to deepen their belief.

2. "Why are you so afraid? Have you still have no faith?" (Mark 4:40). Jesus asked this question to his disciples during a storm at sea, challenging their fear and lack of trust in God's power and strengthening their belief.

3. "Why do you call me 'Lord, Lord,' and not do what I tell you?" (Luke 6:46). Jesus asked this question to emphasize the importance of obedience and genuine discipleship. Belief requires a choice.

4. "Do you want to be healed?" (John 5:6). Jesus asked this question to a man who had been paralyzed for many years, prompting him to consider his desire for healing and his readiness to receive it. The man had first to believe he could be healed.

5. "Do you believe that I am able to do this?" (Matthew 9:28). Jesus asked this question to two blind men who sought healing. He challenged their faith and affirmed their belief in his power to

perform miracles.

Every question is an opportunity to decide something. Jesus asked these **decision** questions to establish and strengthen belief in his followers. When we summon belief, we tap into our inner conviction and faith in something greater than ourselves. It is the unwavering trust that what we desire or strive for is possible and attainable.

Jesus' questions serve as catalysts for spiritual growth challenging us to confront our fears, trust in a higher power, and make deliberate choices. They remind us that belief isn't just a passive state; it's an active force that can be summoned to drive meaningful action.

Similarly, that's how I see belief. It's always there with us, but sometimes it doesn't show itself because we are preoccupied. Belief must be provoked to know it's there, giving us a choice. Once we choose to believe, that's when we discover its power inside us.

Summoning belief involves cultivating a positive mindset and reframing negative self-talk into empowering thoughts. It requires focusing on our strengths, achievements, and past successes as evidence that we can achieve our goals. Doing so can build confidence and bolster our belief in our abilities. Ultimately, by summoning belief, we tap into our inner strength and unlock the potential to achieve remarkable things.

Filling Your Bucket with Belief

By choosing this book, chances are you're yearning to unlock your full potential and find your purpose. Yet, something feels like it's holding you back, like a thick humidity that clouds your vision and dampens your spirit. I understand that feeling all too well. Its stifling force can obscure our true selves and hinder our growth. But what if I told you that the key to clearing that fog lies in the power of belief?

Think again to the story of the Chilean miners, trapped underground, the mine caving in from the top and the bottom, yet driven by unshakable belief in their rescue. Their 'buckets' were filled with the belief that they would survive, and it propelled them to take the necessary steps for survival. Similarly, your 'bucket of belief' can be the catalyst that propels you to break free from what's holding you back and step into your full potential.

The fixed mindset leads to burnout and self-sabotage, often this is brought on by self-doubt and holding on to limiting beliefs because you may feel incapable or undeserving. Over time the feeling of being stuck is detrimental to both your personal and professional life. Instead, fill your bucket with focus and your energy on constructive activities.

***

Many years ago, I suffered from anemia. I walked around with low blood resulting from a chronic medical condition. I had low energy, my mind was always cloudy, and I had little incentive to do anything beyond what I needed. One day, I experienced an unusual amount of bleeding during my menstrual cycle, and I was taken to the hospital.

Medical personnel asked how I had been transported to the hospital and were shocked to learn a friend had driven me. With my fragile condition, they were certain I'd have come by ambulance. You see, my blood level was so low that I was on the verge of congestive heart failure. I was admitted and immediately given blood transfusions. On the day of my release, I skipped out of the hospital. I felt like a new person because I had *blood!*

Here's my point. I had been walking around with low blood for so long that I thought that *was my life* (a fixed mindset if there ever was one). I accepted that I would always have low energy. I am here to tell you, when we know what is weighing us down, we must do everything we can to diagnose our issue, even if it means getting professional help.

Feeling frustrated or stuck is common when we sense we have untapped potential. Sometimes it can even make you physically ill. Reflecting on your goals, passions, and what truly matters to you can provide valuable insights and recharge your motivation. Additionally, seeking support from friends, mentors, or professionals can be beneficial in navigating this journey of self-discovery and personal growth.

Faith and Belief: Intertwining Ropes

We've defined belief as the willingness to act on a certain hypothesis, a proposition rooted in our capacity to exercise free will and trust our judgment. However, belief takes on a profound transformation when we introduce the concept of faith, which offers a more robust option, one grounded in an individual's inherent right to believe in a higher power, a divine source, or God.

The God hypothesis presents us with a genuine choice to believe in the existence of a universal and divine force that transcends human comprehension. When we embrace faith, we extend our belief beyond the limits of our immediate experiences, placing our trust in a higher order that guides and influences our lives in ways that often transcend our understanding.

Belief, while an intangible concept, is far from artificial. It is an intricate tapestry, not something that can be manufactured or imposed on someone. It lies within and reflects our individual perspectives and inner truth. Whether a concept, an idea, or a goal, belief is a genuine and authentic aspect of the human experience, a deeply rooted conviction or faith in something. It often arises from personal experiences, values, knowledge, or a sense of intuition.

For me, belief is closely intertwined with the principle of faith. In fact, although I am presenting many practical aspects of belief as a growth mindset pillar, I firmly believe that belief and faith are closely related concepts, each holding a distinct yet interconnected place in our spiritual journey. In less philosophical terms, belief refers to the acceptance or conviction in the truth or existence of something, often rooted in our understanding, experiences, or knowledge. It's a foundational element upon which faith can be built; I am committed to providing you with a foundation that will help your belief move toward greater faith.

***

While my foundational beliefs are rooted in Christianity, I advocate for an ecumenical approach. We can enrich our own spiritual journeys by learning from the wisdom found in various religious traditions. Each tradition offers a unique lens through which to explore the intricate relationship between belief and faith, and I find these cross-cultural perspectives enlightening and affirming.

- **Christianity (Hebrews 11:1):** "Now faith is confidence in what we hope for and assurance about what we do not see." Faith involves a level of certainty beyond what is visible, akin to a deeper dimension of belief.

— **Islam (Quran 2:286):** "Allah does not burden a soul beyond that it can bear..." Believers place trust and reliance in Allah's wisdom and mercy, based on their beliefs in His attributes.

— **Buddhism (Dhammapada 21:290):** "No one saves us but ourselves. No one can and no one may. We ourselves must walk the path." Personal experience is important, and understanding—or belief—leads to the faith-driven action of walking the path to enlightenment.

— **Judaism (Proverbs 3:5-6):** "Trust in the LORD with all your heart and lean not on your own understanding; in all your ways submit to him, and he will make your paths straight.

Each tradition underscores the universal right we all have to access and express our faith in different ways. These shared themes across different religions highlight the universality of belief and faith, affirming that regardless or our individual paths, we all have the right to fortify our beliefs and deepen our faith in ways that resonate with us.

Richard Rohr in *Wonderous Encounters: Scriptures for Lent,* eloquently states that faith involves 'releasing ourselves into the belly of darkness,' (like Jonah) before we can know what is essential...that the spiritual journey is more like giving up control than taking control,' a surrender that often comes after we've established a strong foundation of belief.

So, as you continue on your own spiritual journey, consider how beliefs can serve as stepping stones to a deeper, more profound faith. It's clear that this concept serves as the bedrock upon which faith can be built. The ropes intertwined establish a strong foundation to nurture a growth mindset.

Belief: Truth in the Making

William James is a classical voice of clarity for me as I endeavor to stretch my thinking. In one of his four essays, "The Will to Believe," he wrote, "There are some beliefs which are truth in the making." I love this because it represents manifestation in action. He adds, "And often enough, our faith beforehand in an uncertified result is the only thing that makes the result come true." In other words, scientific methods, rationality, or your own experiences, in some cases, may not justify your belief.

You can still summon the will to believe! Even without evidence, you *can* believe. There are some beliefs that are truth in the making; for instance, scientific theories that are continually tested and refined. They represent our current understanding and are considered *truth in the making* until further evidence solidifies them. Historical events and their interpretations are another example that can change over time as new evidence or perspectives emerge. Likewise, your beliefs can change as new knowledge and experiences come into play. *Truth in the making* underscores the dynamic and evolving nature of our understanding in our mindset, various fields and domains of knowledge. This profound philosophical idea encapsulates the essence of manifestation and its transformative power. It suggests that certain beliefs—when deeply held and nurtured—can shape our reality and bring forth a previously unseen or unrealized truth.

Manifestation, in its essence, involves aligning our thoughts, beliefs, and intentions with the desired outcomes we wish to bring into existence. It is the conscious act of harnessing the power of our mind and channeling it toward realizing our goals and aspirations. And within this process, belief assumes a pivotal role.

When we embrace a belief with unwavering conviction, it becomes an active force that shapes our perception and influences our actions. By firmly believing in a particular outcome or truth, we create a resonance within ourselves that aligns us with the energy and possibilities necessary to bring that truth to fruition. In this sense, belief becomes the driving force behind the manifestation process.

Often, the manifestation journey begins with envisioning a desired outcome before any concrete evidence or external validation exists. Our unwavering faith in that envisioned result is a catalyst, propelling us toward its realization. Through the power of belief and unwavering faith, we can transcend the boundaries of what may seem possible or probable.

We tap into limitless potential and create a space where our desired outcomes can materialize. The unwavering conviction in the truth we seek to manifest opens doors, unlocks opportunities, and paves the way for its ultimate realization.

Sometimes we must wait for the belief to show up; in many instances it is likely to require patience and time. For instance, we may need more information or circumstances to understand or witness our beliefs' manifestation fully. It can be tempting to become discouraged or give up when things don't happen as quickly as we hope. However, *waiting on belief* suggests that we should exercise patience and maintain our belief, allowing time for things to unfold in their way.

While waiting for belief to materialize, we must remain proactive and take any necessary actions or steps within our control. This might involve learning, planning, and making strategic choices that align with our beliefs, all while understanding that the outcome may take time to materialize. You want that job? Persist and keep upgrading your skills. Praying to start a family? Take care of your health and make plans for the new arrival. Looking to buy a new home? Wait and take care of the one you are currently living in.

Waiting on belief can also be an opportunity for personal growth and self-reflection. It allows us to develop resilience, strengthen our resolve, and deepen our understanding of ourselves and our aspirations. It means holding onto our conviction and trusting that what we believe will eventually come to fruition, even if the process takes longer than expected.

Drawing from the well of belief isn't a one-time act; it is a continuous process that requires us to hold on to our convictions, even when evidence or immediate results are lacking. It's about remaining steadfast, proactive, and patient, allowing time for our deeply held beliefs to materialize into our live reality. So, as you navigate the challenges and opportunities that life presents, remember your well of belief is a reservoir of untapped potential. Keep drawing from it, don't be afraid to fill your bucket to the brim. Your belief is your truth in the making, a catalyst that can unlock doors, create opportunities, and pave the way for your ultimate realization.

Trust and Test:
Bold Steps to Drawing from the Well

Trusting and testing belief has become a regular part of my own journey of personal and professional growth. Years ago, I learned how to manifest my thoughts while working as an Independent Beauty Consultant for Mary Kay Cosmetics. Mary Kay Cosmetics taught me the power of manifesting thoughts into reality. The mantra, *Believe you can succeed*, was more than a tagline; although I am no longer with the company, the mantra became a guiding principle that I've carried with me ever since.

I gained significant experience in qualifying for awards, from strutting across the stage to claim top sales and recruitment honors at the company's annual event, Seminar, to earning a coveted Red Jacket award for team building success. Director was on my radar, a milestone that granted some the privilege of a free car, however, I didn't stay long enough in the business to achieve the illustrious Pink Cadillac status.

My journey involved exploring several home-based MLMs in search of the right fit, and I admit I jumped around quite a bit. Yet, deep down, I hold the belief that if I had persisted and stayed the course, you might have eventually spotted me cruising down the road in my very own Pink Cadillac.

This story is a testament to the power of belief and determination, demonstrating that unwavering commitment, even the most coveted dreams can become a reality. My sales director always encouraged me to work as though everything depended on me and to trust God to take care of the rest.

I have added testing my beliefs to the process. Mary Kay is only one example. Here are a few others in which I've put my beliefs to the test, from navigating the complexities of home loans to making career leaps. Let's take a look!

When my husband and I embarked on the journey to build our first home, we encountered formidable roadblocks along the way. These obstacles ranged from environmental issues, such as the need to cap a well, to stringent scrutiny of our financial situation. Only three years into launching our new family business, we faced the common reality that most business owners do not draw a salary in the early years but reinvest profits into the company's growth. This financial predicament seemed to cast a shadow on our dreams of homeownership, as the house we were constructing appeared to be larger than what our pocketbook could support.

After jumping through hoops to qualify and with the mortgage approval still pending, I confidently told the loan officer, "The home is ours, and now it's up to you and the bank if you want us as customers." I was a banker, so I knew how arrogant this sounded. But I had unwavering belief. I was speaking the outcome into existence. However, in the end, a remarkable transformation occurred, thanks to the unwavering dedication of our loan officers. She went beyond evaluating our present circumstances, delving into our past and her own trust in our future. It was as if divine favor had intervened to guide us through these seemingly insurmountable challenges. Our belief in God and the power of perseverance saw us through, proving that sometimes when we face life's most daunting roadblocks, faith and determination can pave the way to unexpected and miraculous solutions. We were confident because we had done all we knew to do and had decided to leave the rest to God. The mortgage was approved. We received excellent terms and moved into the house with more equity than we'd anticipated.

Trust and testing belief often go hand in hand, as they involve having confidence and faith in something or someone. While belief is a personal conviction or acceptance of something as true, trust is the reliance or dependence we place on someone or something based on our belief in their reliability, integrity, or abilities. Trust is built over time through consistent experiences in which our belief is tested. Putting our beliefs to the test strengthens them. I have had a lot of practice testing my beliefs. Here is another example.

With nearly 20 years in community banking, I was looking for the next step in my career. Fiserv, a financial services company, was practically in my backyard, and I wanted to work for a global company. I drove to the campus frequently, examined the buildings, and told myself I would work there one day. In my visualizations, I was specific about the job and the salary. I kept driving to campus, picturing myself inside, walking the halls, sitting in my office, and having meetings in conference rooms with colleagues, and eating in the employee cafe. I landed another interview after a couple of attempts and was hired shortly after.

***

Belief also serves as my foundation for self-care, a compassionate ally that encourages exploration beyond the boundaries of my comfort zone.

It empowers me to embark on new journeys, navigate my relationship with food, embrace my unique body type, channel creative expression, and cultivate my abilities. With belief as my compass, I curate my values to ensure that my actions align with what truly matters in my life.

This unwavering belief has been the driving force that transformed this manuscript from a rough draft into a completed work. It enabled me not only to appreciate constructive criticism but also to endure numerous edits and rewrites to shape a coherent message. It's my profound faith in these pillars and their capacity to bring about transformative change in our lives that fuels my dedication and exploration.

***

In the hushed moments that gently follow each chapter's exploration of belief, abilities, self-insight, intellect, and spirit, I extend to you a precious gift—a chance to heed my grandmother's wisdom, " Hush A Minute." Back in our bustling childhood days, spending summers with my grandmother, her quest for tranquility amidst the clamor of life often led her to the living room, where the television broadcasted Billy Graham's sermons. With the screen door banging, the ceaseless chatter of my cousins and me, and our frequent trips to the fridge for refreshments, we unwittingly disrupted her moments of serenity.

Yet, in those interruptions, my grandmother wielded a timeless phrase, one that held the power to hush us momentarily and command our attention, much like a conductor silencing a cacophonous orchestra before a grand performance. To her, it was a simple utterance, but in its simplicity lay profound depth—a depth that could still our restless thoughts, center our wandering spirits, and beckon the door to self-discovery wide open.

As we arrive at these reflections, let's embrace the opportunity to be present, to listen to the whispers of our inner selves, and to take to heart the lessons that have unfolded. In these spaces of quiet contemplation, we'll illuminate the pathways to profound insights and transformative growth.

So, as we embark on this collective journey of self-discovery and personal empowerment, won't you join me in hushing a minute? Together, we'll uncover the gems that reside within, weaving the tapestry of our growth story. And remember, for those seeking a deeper dive, additional reflections await in the Appendix of the book.

HUSH A MINUTE

Belief is a pillar that delivers transformative power and is the cornerstone of a growth mindset. We discussed how tapping into your inner well of belief can unleash untapped potential. Belief serves as your passport to personal and professional growth. We explored the symbiotic relationship between belief and faith, emphasizing manifestation and the will to believe, which is crucial for progress. We discussed the need for a balanced approach to trusting and testing belief to wake-up our confidence and allow us to take bold action toward our goals.

I want to encourage you now to begin with setting intention, starting where you are identifying and clarifying what you want to achieve in your life or manifest. Setting intention goes beyond wishful thinking or vague desires; it involves a focused and intentional approach to defining your objectives.

Ask yourself, and listen to your authentic voice.

How can I align my set intentions with a growth mindset?

How can I leverage set intentions to create meaningful progress in my life?

How can I ensure that my set intentions are not merely wished but actionable steps toward personal growth and fulfillment?

Answering these questions allows us to approach our goals with clarity, resilience, and commitment to continuous growth, ultimately empowering us to create meaningful and transformative progress.

CHAPTER TWO

PILLAR # 2: ABILITIES

Jocelyn is a joy to have in class but she talks too much.

2nd Grade Teacher, Garfield Elementary School

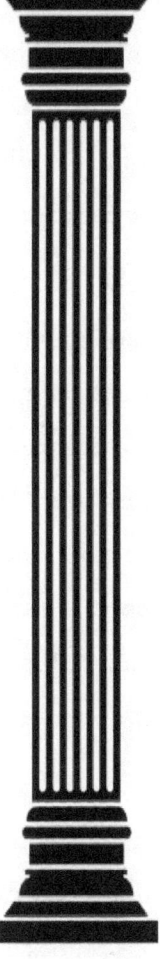

Unlocking Your Inner Wizard: Shifting Paradigms And Embracing Your Abilities

The Wizard of Oz, a cinematic masterpiece that first graced the screens in 1939, has forever captivated my heart and mind. This enduring gem ranks among my favorite films. As a young girl, I reveled in the spectacle and cheered on the protagonists as they valiantly confronted the malevolence woven by the Wicked Witch of the West. Her treacherous schemes, a palpable threat to Dorothy and her companions, held me in suspense, an eager witness to their journey.

Over the passage of time, my connection to the film endured, an enigma I couldn't fully decipher. There was an intangible allure in the characters' quests, a yearning for profound change and realization of potential. The lion's pursuit of courage, the tin man's search for a heart, and the scarecrow's aspiration for a brain–his journey especially resonated with me. Even back then, as the frames flickered, the intricate messages woven beneath the narrative eluded my conscious grasp, leaving an indelible imprint of intrigue.

Much like Dorothy and her friends discovered their inner strengths in the *Wizard of Oz*, we too have abilities that often go unnoticed or underutilized causing us to hide in the shadows. We can pull back the curtain and reveal the real magic that lies within each of us–our unique abilities. Today, I stand on the threshold of enlightenment. My mission is intricately woven with the storytelling of "The Wizard of Oz." The passage of time has led me on a journey of self-discovery, and in its wake, the true significance of this timeless narrative has become vividly apparent. The film has become a guiding star, illuminating the path I was meant to tread.

Reflecting on my years of championing growth and nurturing minds and hearts, I recognize the mirror between the characters' quests and my own mission. Lion's pursuit of courage embodies the empowerment I instill, urging individuals to confront fears and uncertainties head-on. Tin Man sought a heart, just as I have endeavored to awaken the emotional core within those I mentor, encouraging them to embrace their vulnerabilities and strengths alike. Scarecrow's yearning for a brain mirrors my dedication to fostering intellectual growth and self-awareness, aligning with the pillars I've so passionately shared.

The film's essence, entwined with my own journey, underscores the significance of each step taken, every insight shared, and every individual empowered. The profound substance I seek in my interactions echoes in the transformative layers of *The Wizard of Oz*, guiding me forward with a newfound depth of understanding and conviction.

***

I haven't got a brain…only straw.

Scarecrow (before receiving his diploma from the Wizard), The Wizard of Oz, 1939.

At the start of his journey, Scarecrow is plagued by self-doubt, convinced that he lacks the brain and intellect to face challenges. However, his actions throughout the story reveal the inherent fallacy in his belief. His creativity, resourcefulness, and clever problem-solving all showcase his remarkable abilities. As he overcomes each obstacle, he showcases the intelligence he thought he lacked.

In the climax of his story, when he receives his "diploma," it becomes evident that he had the capacity to think critically all along. This pivotal moment resonates with the growth mindset's 'ability' pillar, illuminating that belief in one's capabilities can catalyze remarkable transformation. Scarecrow's evolution exemplifies the realization that a proper growth mindset involves recognizing, nurturing, and leveraging one's abilities to their fullest potential.

As we've explored, the true wizardry isn't in some external force but within ourselves. Recognizing and harnessing our abilities can be transformative, turning the ordinary into the extraordinary. Just like Scarecrow you have the power; you just need to realize it.

Shifting Perspectives:
The New Lens on Abilities

The sum of the square roots of any two sides of an isosceles triangle is equal to the square root of the remaining side.

Scarecrow (after he receives his diploma from the Wizard), The Wizard of Oz, 1939.

Sometimes, our abilities are hidden, not because they don't exist but because we're looking at them through a distorted lens. Recollections of my primary school years brought to light moments when my second-grade teacher complained about my excessive chatter. Each report card bore the refrain, "Jocelyn is a joy to have in the classroom, but she talks too much." At the time, my mother would smile knowingly, the words seeming on each report card echoing the last.

Over time, though, Mom's smile turned into a frown. The teacher's ink seemed to surrender to monotony, merely writing "same as before." The last and final time these words were written, my mother promptly enrolled me in another school.

As I reflect now, the memory of my ceaseless talking invites contemplation. Was my chatter aimed at disruption, challenging the teacher's authority? Or was it merely excessive sociability? Yet, what if my loquaciousness had been channeled? Could it have been a reservoir of leadership potential, fueling endeavors like guiding classmates in creative pursuits, donning the role of a classroom monitor, or orchestrating harmonious order? This would have required looking at my talking "too much" in a new light.

How might a different approach have transformed my chatter from a perceived flaw into a unique ability? Just as Scarecrow's quest for a brain in *The Wizard of Oz* led him to discover his latent intellect, a paradigm shift could have steered my prattle towards productivity. Similarly, as Scarecrow's journey unmasked his potential, so too could my chatter, if harnessed wisely, bring my leadership abilities to their full fruition.

Scientific research has found that most people are born with innate abilities, natural talents, and aptitudes. These abilities include intelligence, creativity, and physical strength, mainly genetic in nature and primarily determined at birth. Like intelligence, ability must be developed, nurtured, tested, and exercised. I believe God gave us abilities to apply them to our purpose. As stewards of our abilities, we engage and grow them to make a difference in the world while doing what God has called us to do while on earth.

Dr. Carol Dweck suggests that there are differences between someone with a growth mindset and a learner vs. a non-learner. She asks, "What on earth would make someone a non-learner? Everyone is born with an intense drive to learn. Infants stretch their skills daily. Not just ordinary skills but the most difficult tasks of a lifetime, like learning to walk and talk. They never decide it's too hard or not worth the effort. Babies don't worry about humiliating themselves. They walk, they fall, they get up."

So, what happens as we mature? Do we lose our abilities? Heck no! It's not about losing them; it's about wasting them. Wasted abilities are those skills and talents we possess but fail to develop or use. They are talents and skills that fade away as we progress through life. This is either because we don't carve out the time or summon the energy to pursue them, or we don't see them as important. As life bogs us down, we forget them, bury them, stomp on them, or allow someone else to do so. In the end, we decide that further development is not worthwhile. In *Growth Mindset: The Unstoppable You,* life Coach, Marcus Johanssen, cautions us that self-imposed limitations "are not what you can't do, but what you believe you can't do."

***

Take a moment to journey back in time and recollect an instance when you dared to push your limits, when the boundaries of your capabilities were surpassed. Your achievements danced far beyond the realms of your imagination. Can you conjure the sensations? Did they resemble the unfurling of a blossom, the refreshing embrace of a rain shower, or the triumphant ascent to a summit? As I ponder this, I'm reminded of Scarecrow's transformation when he achieved feats that defied his own perceptions—a surge of confidence that resonates deeply.

Much like Scarecrow, these remarkable moments are wellsprings of empowerment, infusing us with newfound assurance. I invite you to relive that exhilarating feeling. Just as Scarecrow's feats emboldened him, so can your recollections propel you forward. Illuminate the path ahead with memories of past triumphs, for they stand as a testament to the boundless potential within. Changing how we view our abilities can be as impactful as discovering new ones. A paradigm shift doesn't just change what you see; it changes how you see, opening up new avenues for growth and self-discovery.

The Essence of Being:
Abilities as a State of Mind

Let's be real. Embracing a growth mindset doesn't equate to overlooking areas that may require nurturing. Yet, avoiding the trap of self-flagellation for these imperfections is vital. Punishing oneself due to perceived imperfections is akin to tethering oneself to a fixed mindset. You can address these aspects without allowing them to hinder your progress. Imperfections are subtle tugs from the divine, reminders of the constant presence of a guiding force. I liken them to birthmarks, distinct marks that set us apart from the crowd and directly link us to the Creator; therefore, they have meaning and purpose.

We, every single one of us, are exquisite works of art adorned with flaws. However, these imperfections don't diminish our worth but underline it. They are like brushstrokes, adding character and authenticity to the canvas of our existence. Just as an artist doesn't discard a masterpiece due to a singular flaw– sometimes that flaw becomes their signature, a symbol of their identity. These marks render us authentic and unparalleled, turning us into masterpieces that bear the unique touch of the Creator.

This journey calls for trust and unwavering belief, to cease whispering to ourselves that our abilities are lacking merely because some paths demand effort. Consider this: there's not a single person who leans solely on their talent. Success, in every realm, fuses talent with dedication. It's a symphony in which the notes of hard work harmonize with our innate gifts, each resonating to create the masterpiece of achievement.

Comparing oneself to those gifted in different ways leads to self-doubt. Ease isn't synonymous with superiority. Effortless perfection is a myth. Each of us bears a role that no one else can fulfill. The world eagerly anticipates your arrival on the stage of your journey, a stage where showing up for yourself is not a mere option but an obligation.

In this odyssey of growth, recognize the realms of knowledge yet to be explored. Acknowledging your limitations is a stepping stone to broader horizons, paving the way for true understanding and evolution. It's a process that might be painful, yet this very discomfort serves as a crucible for transformation.

Each conflict encountered, each struggle endured, presents an opportunity for growth. When harnessed, these trials become conduits for inner strength, sculpting your character into a force of resilience.

Granting space for these encounters tempers and propels you to evolve beyond yourself. In this tapestry of life, growth arises not only from the triumphs but also from the shadows, for they contribute to the masterpiece that you, uniquely, are crafting. Understanding that abilities extend beyond skills and talents to include how we perceive ourselves and our potential allows us to approach life holistically. When we embrace the 'ability to be' we unlock a deeper level of self-awareness and empowerment.

HUSH A MINUTE

The Abilities Pillar holds that we are born with innate abilities, natural talents, aptitudes, and natural strength, mainly genetic in nature and primarily determined at birth. However, like intelligence, ability must be developed, nurtured, tested, and exercised. As stewards of our abilities, we engage and grow them to make a difference in the world while fulfilling our individual purpose on earth.

Ask yourself…listen to your authentic voice.

What are my innate talents and abilities?

What steps can I take to develop and enhance these abilities?

How can I align my abilities with my personal goals and aspirations?

CHAPTER THREE

PILLAR #3 SELF-INSIGHT

COME TO YOUR SENSES

There is only one Truth and as you go looking for it through the forest of seeking be careful lest you bump into a tree.

That lump on your head may remind you that everything is God.

You are like a forest dweller looking for the forest.

What am I to do?

Listen, friend, each crackling leaf beneath your feet is a personal invitation to come to your senses.

Has it occurred to you that you are seeking God with His eyes?

~Adyashan

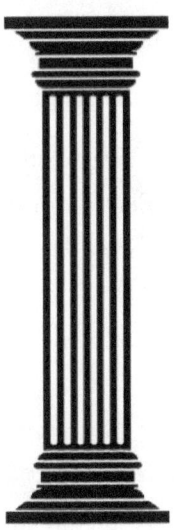

Discovering Your Secret Sauce: Self Insight

For many years, my mom was the culinary heart of our home. However, the aftermath of two strokes has prevented her from continuing her role as the family chef. Taking up the mantle, I initially felt the weight of her gastronomic legacy. But with time and patience, and a willingness to experiment, I've found my groove in the kitchen and have even started to surprise myself with my own creative flair. I have crafted my own "secret sauce," both in the literal sense and as a metaphor for my newfound confidence.

In a similar manner, my own unique flavors and values provide the essential ingredients in the recipe of life. They guide me, much like a culinary compass, on this enriching journey of self -discovery. You, too, have a unique blend of qualities, experiences, and perspectives that make you who you are. Self-insight is the special ingredient that distinguishes you from the anyone else.

While preparing a delicious meal to make others happy has its own joy, my quest to please people has often been my downfall. I've faced emotional struggles in my attempts to be something that didn't align with my true self. Over time, though, I have found that one of the biggest benefits of self-insight is the freedom from conforming to fit in or please others. I've learned to embrace my core beliefs without sacrificing my integrity.

Having hidden under a persona for so long, I was open to finding out how to rewrite my expectations, rethink what I assumed, and let go of ideas that no longer fit me. In fact, I work every day on unlearning things that just flat-out don't make any sense. I can set the standards, create my own path, and be unapologetically myself through self-reflection and awareness.

The Recipe for Self-Insight

Self-insight is like creating your own secret sauce of self-understanding. This introspective journey serves as the formula for crafting a life that is not just fulfilling but uniquely yours. This kind of awareness is an introspective process of understanding and recognizing oneself. It involves recognizing our strengths, weaknesses, beliefs, values, and emotions and how they shape our identities.

When we turn the lens inward, peeling back the layers of our psyche, we discover hidden motivations and untapped aspirations. Just as a unique blend of ingredients can elevate a dish, this deep self-awareness enriches our lives, adding a flavor that is distinctly our own. The outer self is the reflection of your inner thoughts and emotions, so its beneficial to understand yourself.

Reflect and Connect. Getting to know yourself is akin to studying the meanings of your existence. It's a deep dive into the framework of your emotions, thoughts, and behaviors that collectively define who you are. Recently, I've spent more time pondering my priorities, assessing my current situation, uncovering hidden aspects of myself, and trying to figure out my ultimate purpose. Whether it's taking a step back from a demanding job to focus on family, realizing that quality time with loved ones is a top priority, assessing one's health in order to gain increased energy and happiness, or exploring a newfound passion for painting (for me, it's finally being able to concentrate on my writing), these reflections serve as my personal blueprint for crafting a life that is fulfilling and uniquely me.

Self- insight fosters a closer connection with our true selves, empowering us to live more authentically. The more you understand your inner workings, the better equipped you are to navigate life's complexities. Your self-insight serves as your personal blueprint, guiding you toward a more fulfilling life.

Identify and thrive. Our sense of identity is strengthened through self-insight. By embracing our authentic essence, we shed societal expectations. We cultivate a sense of self that transcends external judgments and definitions when we recognize our unique qualities, passions, and values. As we become more aware of ourselves, we become more capable of navigating the complexities of personal growth.

Catch and release potential. In order to embark on a transformational journey of continuous development, self-insight catalyzes personal growth. We can harness our potential and work towards self-improvement. Our inner journey combined with a growth mindset, empowers us to embrace challenges, seek new opportunities, and learn from them. As a result, we will be able to step outside of our comfort zones, take calculated risks, and adapt to changing circumstances.

Cultivate organic growth. A person's sense of self is shaped by their unique experiences and perspectives. The things that bring insight and growth to one person may not be the same for another. The relative nature of self-insight emphasizes the importance of individuality and diversity in personal growth. Appreciating the relative nature of self-insight fosters empathy, understanding, and respect for others' journeys.

Live authentically. A deep understanding of your own thoughts, feelings, and behaviors, serves as a powerful tool. When you are aware of your own emotional triggers, you become better equipped to recognize similar patterns in others. This is the understanding that allows you to "put yourself in someone else's shoes."

This type of self-insight leads to greater emotional intelligence and social awareness. Developing self-insight helps embolden our truth. We can live authentically and be resilient to competing values when we understand ourselves better. By developing self-insight, we open the door to personal growth, challenge societal norms, and reshape our future.

To Thine Own Self Be True: The Final Act

Shakespeare's timeless wisdom, "To thine own self be true," serves as a guiding principle for many. Personally, it ranks at the top of my 'words to live by' because it speaks to authenticity. Self-insight is a reliable pillar to guide my growth, honoring my identity while staying focused on what truly matters. By nurturing our self-insight, we can make a positive impact on the world.

Embracing my journey, unburdened by comparisons, has been liberating. I've become aware that the brilliance of individuality dims when contrasted with others. Wisdom, shaped by experience, sharpens judgment and unveils truths. This synergy breeds growth, empathy, and wise choices.

Self-awareness anchors success on your terms. The aim isn't to achieve a flawless version of yourself, but rather to focus on evolving through your distinct set of strengths. It's about recognizing what you naturally excel at and leveraging those abilities to propel yourself forward. This approach not only fosters personal growth but also builds a sense of authenticity and self-acceptance.

I love to meet interesting people because being interesting doesn't merely attract; it inspires. Cultivating curiosity, exploring life, and sharing insights create a magnetic persona. Through these fascinating personalities, I have learned that staying true to your values is necessary for authenticity to radiate. Unwavering values shape our path, inviting experiences aligned with our true self. We can define success on our own terms. Embrace dreams, passions, and aspirations, forging a journey of growth, empowerment, and purpose.

I urge you to celebrate your distinctiveness—talents, experiences, and all. Prioritize growth, learning, and progress over external validation. Step into your full potential, free from the chains of others' judgments. Being true to yourself is the ultimate act of self-insight.

Unlocking an Abundant Life Through Self-Insight: Becoming Your Best Self

Scripture informs us that, those who share their talents are promised abundance (Matthew 25:29). Embrace self-insight to become the best version of yourself, fully and authentically. Applying this knowledge fosters a connection to your true self.

Since relocating to Arizona, the great outdoors has become my new sanctuary (when it is not 120°), in stark contrast to my life in Wisconsin. It amazes me how nature effortlessly exists in its purest form. Despite the harshness of the desert, I am struck by its stark beauty, the rock formations, cacti, succulents, and the desert sky at night, all intricately designed by the Creator.

The experience of Mother nature has taught me how to weather the storms, that for everything that happens in my life, there is a season, and with each new season come new beginnings, challenges and triumphs. Through the steady flow of streams, I learn how to persevere despite obstacles, and through the variety of plant life, I discover how to embrace my own unique qualities and strengths. As the elements that surround me teach me, my potential for growth and transformation is limitless. These profound lessons nurture my best self.

Nature bestows upon us sunlight and starlight. If the sun were a personality, she would radiate her brilliance, casting her energy without reservations, leaving no corner untouched. When the sun reigns, darkness has no refuge. In contrast, the stars inhabit spaces scattered across the night's canvas, sprinkling their luminance amidst the darkness. I see myself as akin to starlight, paving a path for you to step out from the shadows and shine your own light through the boundless potential within you. Our most authentic self can be unlocked by acknowledging and using the unique traits God has bestowed on us.

This newfound awareness has been transformative. Rather than scattering my focus across multiple endeavors (a trait my friends were quick to notice), I'm now more intentional about where to focus my energy. Instead of getting entangled in draining activities, I've made a conscious shift towards directing my energy into endeavors that resonate deeply with my goals and values. For instance, I am currently in a season when I've prioritized caregiving for my mother. This transformation enables me to allocate my time and emotional resources wisely, affording me the opportunity to wholeheartedly invest in a role that harmonizes seamlessly with my core values and priorities.

This targeted approach not only boosts my productivity in other interests but also enhances my well-being. I am learning how to practice self-care without feeling guilty. It's like knowing exactly where to plant seeds in a garden for the most bountiful harvest. By being intentional with my energy, I'm better equipped to grow in the directions that matter most to me.

Spending time getting to know yourself helps you to recognize your worth and know where to invest it. Gaining self-insight empowers you to navigate when to engage and when to step back. Some people and situations don't deserve your energy, a lesson I've learned through my own experiences.

How can you do this? It can be challenging to be both the subject and the object of your own life story, actively participating while also having the wisdom to pause, reflect, and adjust course when needed. The idea of seeing inside the self is a paradoxical concept, but it's often addressed through introspection. Think of it as stepping back mentally to observe your thoughts, feelings and actions as if you were an external observer.

This can be challenging because it requires detaching from your immediate experiences to gain a more objective view. When you do this, you can take stock of your biases, judgments and pre-conceived notions. Techniques like mindfulness, meditation, and journaling can help in this process by creating the mental space needed to "see" inside yourself more clearly.

This pillar of the growth mindset is an anchor, harmonizing priorities and self-care. It helps me maintain balance and allows me time for nurturing my mind, body, and soul. Knowing when to pause for rejuvenation, I am connected with my purpose. This concept infuses intention and significance into our actions, turning tasks into meaningful contributions.

Knowing yourself and why you are here aligns values, passions, and strengths in daily pursuits, yielding a purpose-driven, fulfilling life, which, in turn, unlocks potential and elevates satisfaction. I treasure the freedom to be myself, and self-insight is my compass. Embracing this freedom liberates us from societal pressures, allowing us to embrace our uniqueness without fear.

Your journey of self-insight is like perfecting that secret sauce–each ingredient, each experience, each moment of self-reflection adds depth and flavor to who you are. As you continue to explore your inner landscape, remember that this is an ongoing process, one that will continue to enrich your life in ways you can't even imagine yet.

The Silver Screen of Self-Insight: Lessons from the 'Imitation of Life'

My desire is to be a force for positive change in the world, and writing is my tool for achieving that. As author Mary Pipher puts it, "writing serves to build bridges and inspire meaningful conversations and actions." What really fuels me is the exploration of my own identity and seeing myself in others' stories, and uncovering truths to help solve real world problems.

The gift delivered through self-insight can help the world overcome systemic barriers to acceptance and inclusivity. Systemic issues, like discrimination, inequality, and prejudice, undoubtedly create formidable obstacles that impede our ability to grow and develop spiritually. Through self-insight we acquire the tools to directly address and overcome these challenges. By delving into our biases and prejudices, we can actively engage in the process of dismantling them.

Self-insight acts as a catalyst for a proactive examination of societal norms, allowing us to challenge oppressive structures and advocate for justice and equity. This empowerment enables us to confront systemic barriers head-on, not only within ourselves but also within the broader societal framework. The transformative potential of self-insight turns us into agents of positive change, fostering inclusivity and equality.

***

It's a common belief that art imitates life, and movies frequently serve as mirrors to societal norms and challenges. One such film, a personal favorite of mine from 1959 and still considered and archetype to this day, is *The Imitation of Life*. Through this cinematic masterpiece we can delve into the profound impact of self-insight in our journey to confront and ultimately dismantle systemic barriers.

The melodrama serves as a vivid illustration of characters ensnared within societal expectations, their personal growth stifled by a lack of self-awareness and emotional intelligence. Zooming in on two pivotal characters and their journeys in the movie's latter half, I'm reminded of how their experiences mirror the transformative impact that self-insight can have in breaking free from societal constraints.

Annie Johnson, a widow who is Black, and Lora Meredith, a single mother who is white with dreams of an acting career, form a relationship in the film. They both have daughters around the same age. Annie becomes Lora's housekeeper and later her business partner. The nurturing mother-figure archetype is embodied by Annie. Her desire to help her bi-racial daughter Sarah Jane accept the limits imposed on her by society drives this character's actions. Annie urges Sarah Jane to embrace their perceived inferior economic status, submitting instead, to spiritual elevation.

Sarah Jane rejects her mother's acquiescence and attempts to pass for white, hiding her Blackness while yearning to experience the privileges and opportunities white individuals enjoy. Her longing for material success and acceptance reflects the complexities and challenges she faces as a Black woman in a society marked by racial discrimination.

The film depicts Sarah Jane's struggle to fit into a world that subordinates her true identity. Her character embodies marginalized individuals' dilemmas, forced to hide their authentic selves to assimilate into society. This reality exists in the current day. Their story explores the tension between societal expectations and the longing for self-realization. I don't accept that Sarah Jane's attempts to pass as white should be viewed solely as a mere aspiration for material gains. If we peel back the layers, we will find her yearning to break free from the limitations imposed by a society that unfairly judges individuals based on race.

Her actions underscore the profound impact of systemic racism and the pressures faced by individuals seeking recognition and equality. Her desire to access the opportunities and privileges afforded to white individuals is juxtaposed with her desire to find her place in a privileged society for some and oppressive for others. Systemic barriers have a way of limiting the possibility of thinking under oppressive circumstances. Sarah Jane's aspirations reflect the longing for recognition, acceptance, and equality that individuals in marginalized communities experience.

She cannot appreciate her inherent brilliance and potential and is counting on material success to validate her.

The struggle Sarah Jane faces in the film, echoes the pervasive issue of inequities, marginalization and 'other than' that remains a reality despite the progress that has been made. This particularly affects women and, even more, women of color. Despite advancements, women still encounter systemic barriers in the workplace and society at large, which often manifest as gender bias, misrecognition, and cultural stereotypes. This not only limits professional growth but also impacts their self-perception and self-worth.

The expectation to conform to societal norms or corporate cultures can lead to a form of isolation, where women feel they must suppress their true selves to fit in. This can result in a cycle where women, like the fictional character Sarah Jane, seek external validation through material success rather than recognizing their inherent value and potential.

This juxtaposition between Annie's resigned acceptance, and Sarah Jane's attempts to pass for white shines a light on the complexities of identity and the consequences of systemic racism. It underscores the urgent need for a growth mindset that empowers individuals to embrace their true selves and challenges societal structures perpetuating discrimination and inequality.

It is important to acknowledge that a growth mindset goes beyond personal development; it encompasses a commitment to dismantling systemic barriers and fostering inclusivity. On the surface, Sarah Jane's desire to pass for white and the pursuit of material success overshadows her true desire for equality and the opportunity to live authentically, free from the constraints of racism.

Some film critics give credit to the filmmaker's attempts at posturing an anti-racist point of view. I am hard-pressed to believe that the filmmakers had any social justice motives for making the movie, rather, more of an ideological, stereotypical, and exploitive view of what filmmakers thought about Blacks' place in society in the 1950s. The film still resonates decades later and calls upon us to reflect on systemic inequalities' profound impact and work collectively to create a world where everyone can embrace their true selves.

My perspective on the underlying messages in this film is meant to evoke thinking about how self-insight equips us with a stronger sense of identity, facilitating personal growth and confronting systemic barriers. A closer look exposes the transformative influence of a growth mindset and the ability to confront systemic barriers that hinder our development. The timeless classic serves as a mirror, reflecting the societal barriers that many still face today.

Through self-insight, we can challenge these norms and work towards a more equitable society. We must learn to leverage self-insight to know who we are, live a purposeful life, embrace growth, and navigate societal challenges. There's no need to be someone we're not, hide behind a persona, or seek validation from others.

HUSH A MINUTE

Ask yourself…listen to your authentic voice.

What methods or practices resonate with me for introspection?

What recent experiences, actions or emotions do I feel compelled to delve deeper into?

How can I incorporate regular moments of introspection into my daily or weekly routine?.

CHAPTER FOUR

PILLAR #4 INTELLECT

I have always worshipped at the shrine of knowledge knowing that regardless of how much I study, read, travel, expose myself to enriching experiences, I still remain an intellectual pauper.

- Adam Clayton Powell, Jr.

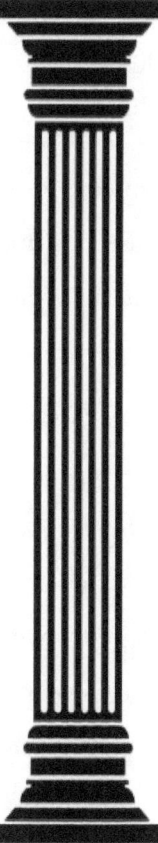

The Multifaceted Nature of Intellect

Intellect is often construed as mere intelligence or the accumulation of knowledge. However, it's much more nuanced than that. Intellect is the ability to think critically, to question deeply, and to connect disparate pieces of information into a cohesive understanding of the world around us. It's not just about knowing facts but is also about understanding the "why" and "how" behind them. It's about being open to new ideas, being willing to challenge your own beliefs, and being humble enough to admit when you don't know something.

***

I felt a tap on my shoulder as I sat at the long dining table in the restaurant, waiting for the pizza we'd ordered for my graduation party. "What have you learned?" the inquisitor asked. "I learned how much I don't know," I said. The depth of humility in my response permeated my words, and I felt it's power.

Adam Grant refers to this concept as "intellectual humility," highlighting the difference between viewing knowledge as power and recognizing the wisdom in acknowledging what we don't know. Knowledge refers to the information, facts, and understanding that a person possesses. It involves the "what" and "why" about various subjects or topics. Intellect, on the other hand, refers to a person's capacity for thinking, reasoning, and problem-solving. Intellect goes beyond mere knowledge and involves the application of knowledge to make decisions, and engage in abstract thinking. It's a shift from equating knowledge with authority to valuing awareness of our own limitations.

In the words of Adam Clayton Powell, Jr., "I am an intellectual pauper." The agony and ecstasy of scholarship have indebted me to "knowing." The truth is–embracing this perspective has liberated me from the constraining persona of trying to be an all-knowing "intellectual." I am on the lookout for learning experiences that stretch my worldview. I relish in my freedom to abide by the joy of learning.

It's funny. Looking back– when I graduated from high school, I distinctly remember telling my mother, "I don't care if I ever stepped foot in another classroom." *I was through with school!* My resignation quickly shifted when I realized the importance of acquiring advanced critical thinking and problem-solving skills. I recognized that to progress in my career, I needed a deeper understanding of business processes and communication.

To cultivate different ways of thinking, I embarked on a journey to delve into various disciplines that demanded higher education. Interestingly, I discovered that many of the roles I aspired to required, at a minimum, a Bachelor's degree. So, I decided to attend college, and to my surprise, I found that that the thirst for learning knew no bounds. This marked the beginning of my transformation into a lifelong learner.

Warren Buffet, a renowned figure in the business world, eloquently advocates this principle. He astutely emphasizes that embracing the path of perpetual learning empowers us to make more informed decisions, recognize novel opportunities, and adapt nimbly to the constantly evolving landscape of our time. By adopting this mindset, we become better equipped to navigate the complexities of our personal and professional lives.

Within the ever-evolving fabric of our world, new and intricate challenges are bound to surface, necessitating imaginative and groundbreaking solutions continually. Each piece of information is a building block that contributes to constructing a more profound and comprehensive understanding of the world.

Cultivating a Future Focused Mindset

Clinging to a static mindset inevitably leads to stagnation and renders us obsolete in the face of progress. A rigid mindset ill-suited to fluidity and change shackles our ability to respond effectively. Hence, our role as shapers of the future is to sow the seeds of flexibility to nurture minds capable of navigating uncharted waters without trepidation. We are challenged to think and rethink, better, slower, question our assumptions and foster a paradigm that breeds problem solvers, shaping a legacy of relevance for future generations.

Every day, every hour, every minute, the world unveils unforeseen challenges, often different from those that preceded them. The next generation must also learn to think critically and draw from a wellspring of wisdom when faced with the unfamiliar. The wisdom, accumulated through learning and life experiences, is the compass that steers us through turbulent seas, enabling us to harness our intellect and intuition in unison.

We are witnessing circumstances and situations we've not been confronted with before. In a world where the only constant is change, our commitment to generating problem solvers echoes as an investment in the evolution of humanity itself. By instilling the tools to grapple with the unknown in the next generation, we ripple into the future with the capacity to surmount hurdles yet to manifest. Each generation we inspire contributes to a legacy of resilience, adaptability, and a ceaseless pursuit of understanding.

One of my greatest delights is being in a classroom with a group of students when they experience "lightbulb" moments. I can almost see the gears turning in their brains. To offer wisdom and thinking processes to this generation is one of my greatest fulfillments.

The canvas of existence is forever splashed with new hues of challenge. To remain relevant, we must evolve in our thinking, nurturing individuals who can wield analytical prowess and wisdom to navigate uncharted territories. Our legacy lies in crafting a lineage of adaptable thinkers who approach the unknown with curiosity, courage, and an innate ability to transcend challenges.

I possess a bias in favor of higher education* to meet these challenges, however, there are numerous ways to embrace lifelong learning and create a lineage of adaptable thinkers, whether through online courses, workshops, reading or attending seminars. Additionally, the arts promote a sense of creativity and curiosity. Diverse experiences such as volunteering can broaden one's outlook, and networking provides exposure to different perspectives and opportunity. Regardless of the means, we should embrace an approach that fosters the growth of adaptable thinkers, equipping them to excel in a constantly evolving world.

*I encountered thoughts that had never crossed my mind before, and learned systems and processes to think better, and I met interesting people

***

"Epistemology," was one of the first unfamiliar words I came across in graduate school. As soon as I learned how to pronounce it, I enjoyed hearing myself say it. Epistemology is the theory of knowledge that concerns us with how, what, and when we can know things. Through it, we study the conditions of truth, belief, and justification.

Epistemology fosters intellectual curiosity, encourages creativity, and nurtures a growth mindset indispensable for personal development and success. Moreover, it instills a sense of humility, reminding us that no matter how much we learn, there will always be more to explore and discover.

As I tread along the path of perpetual learning, I remain committed to embracing new challenges and exploring diverse fields of knowledge.

I understand that the journey may not always be easy, but it is undeniably rewarding and enriching. With every new piece of knowledge, I equip myself with a new lens through which to view the world, broadening my perspectives and enhancing my capacity to contribute positively to society. The same opportunity is relevant for you!

The Boundaries and Horizons of Knowing

You may be wondering, what *can* we know? For an answer, I turn to the ancient Greek philosopher Socrates. He is known for his contributions to the field of epistemology. Socrates' philosophical approach and methods provide insight into that query. The philosopher is famous for his Socratic method, the dialectical questioning aimed at stimulating critical thinking and uncovering underlying assumptions.

Through this method, he engages in dialogues with individuals, skillfully crafting questions that act like a detective's magnifying glass, ready to uncover the fine print of their knowledge and beliefs. I love the playful intellectual ping-pong found in Plato's dialogues – it's like a mental pickleball match.

In Plato's "Apology," Socrates goes all mysterious with his inner voice, which he calls a *daimonion* (divine energy, acting as an inward mentor or demon-antagonist). It's like his personal advice columnist – a sort of philosophical Siri. He describes it as a constant companion, the ultimate wingman of the ancient world, never telling him what to do, but always giving him that "I wouldn't do that if I were you" vibe. So, if you catch yourself deep in conversation with your inner muse, fear not– you're in the esteemed company of Socrates, even if you're just practicing your deep thoughts in the shower (though, maybe save the out-loud version for debates during your shampoo routine).

In doing so, Socrates highlights the importance of recognizing our own ignorance and the necessity of continuous inquiry to gain true understanding. Socrates' key insight into "what we can know" revolves around the concept of "I know that I am ignorant" or "I know that I know nothing." This declaration reflects his belief that genuine wisdom comes from acknowledging our lack of absolute knowledge and our ongoing pursuit of understanding.

He emphasizes that true knowledge involves understanding the underlying principles, questioning assumptions, and engaging in critical thinking. Socrates' teachings also focus on ethics and the examination of one's own values and actions. He believes that self-knowledge and awareness are crucial for leading a virtuous life.

By constantly questioning and examining ourselves, our beliefs, and our actions, we can strive to align our lives with the pursuit of wisdom and virtue. In essence, Socrates' insights guide us to a humble recognition of the limitations of our knowledge while urging us to engage in continuous intellectual exploration and self-examination. He teaches us that the path to wisdom involves acknowledging our ignorance, asking probing questions, and actively seeking to expand our understanding through rigorous inquiry and critical thinking.

Intellectual Agility:
The Heart of a Growth Mindset

My graduate school journey taught me that pursuing knowledge is not a destination but a transforming voyage. By eschewing the notion of being *puffed up* (1 Corinthians 8:1) with knowledge we can embrace the humility that comes with knowing there is always more to learn. This approach liberates us from the constraints of preconceived notions and passionately guides us on a journey of continuous learning.

As we delve into the realm of continuous growth and learning, our consciousness expands, and we become more attuned to the intricacies of the world around us. We develop a heightened awareness of diverse perspectives and understand the interconnectedness of ideas and knowledge across various domains. This expanded consciousness enables us to see beyond the surface and delve deeper into the underlying patterns and complexities that shape our reality.

The intellectual growth mindset empowers us to be proactive in our lives. We take ownership of our personal development and seek new experiences, challenges, and learning opportunities. We welcome feedback and criticism as valuable sources of improvement rather than viewing them as threats to our ego**. This willingness to learn and evolve propels us forward on a path of continuous improvement and self-actualization.

***that voice that says, "you should know this, why don't you?" Or, the one that says, "I know all I need to know."*

The potential for learning resides within each and every one of us, waiting to be unlocked. The yearning for knowledge is a cornerstone of humanity, and it's a wish that I hold dearly, that this thirst for learning could be universally embraced. Unfortunately, forces that want to limit what information is available and to whom, seek to ban books in our educational system. This action has several implications: First, it limits the scope of ideas and perspectives students are exposed to, and this can stifle thinking and intellectual growth. Next, it can perpetuate a narrow worldview, often reflecting the biases or ideologies of those in power who decide what gets banned. Finally, it can be viewed as a form of censorship that hampers both individual and collective learning and development.

The sheer magnitude of ignorance that still lingers in today's world is perplexing. When I reflect on the struggles and triumphs that have shaped our history, all those arduous battles fought to pave the way for education and enlightenment, I'm overwhelmed by a surge of emotion. It's a profound reminder of how far we've come and how much further we can go, fueled by the power of learning and the boundless potential it brings.

Armed with a growth-oriented intellect, we become architects of our destiny. We avoid a passive approach to life and take decisive action to shape our future according to our aspirations and goals. This mindset encourages us to take calculated risks, explore uncharted territories, and embrace the unknown with confidence and resilience.

Furthermore, the intellect growth mindset instills in us a sense of empathy and humility. As we encounter others on their unique journeys, we become more understanding and compassionate, recognizing that everyone is at a different stage of their intellectual evolution. We appreciate the value of collaboration and diverse perspectives, understanding that collective growth is more powerful than individual advancement.

When I think about the impact of a growth-oriented mindset, my women heroes *"SHE-roes"* inspire me. The principles described are embodied by African-American abolitionist and women's rights activist **Sojourner Truth.** Armed with a growth-oriented intellect before a name was assigned to it, Truth refused to accept the passive role assigned to her as a Black woman in a time of pervasive inequality. She became an architect of her destiny by taking decisive action to shape her future and inspire change.

Truth's famous *Ain't I a Woman?* speech (1851) showcased her confidence and resilience as she challenged prevailing gender and racial biases. " Then they talk about this thing in the head; what's this they call it? [member of audience whispers, 'intellect']. That's it, honey. What's that got to do with women's rights or Negroes' rights? If my cup won't hold but a pint and yours holds a quart, wouldn't you be mean not to let me have my little haft measure full?"

Her willingness to embrace the unknown and speak out against injustice demonstrated her determination to explore uncharted territories. Through her advocacy for abolition and women's rights, Truth paved the way for societal transformation, using her intellect and courage to become a beacon of empowerment and change.

Pioneers like **Maria Montessori** (1870-1952) an Italian educator and physician, embodied the intellect growth mindset through her innovative educational philosophy. She said, "It is true that we cannot make a genius. We can only give to each child the chance to fulfill his potential possibilities." She opened the first Montessori school in Rome, in 1907.

Her approach emphasized understanding each child's individual development stage and unique intellectual evolution. Montessori's method fostered empathy and humility in educators by encouraging them to respect the diverse growth journeys of their students. She believed in the value of collaboration between students and teachers, creating an environment where collective growth and mutual learning were paramount.

An intellectual growth mindset allows us to think boldly and broadly, giving birth to our own growth and expanded consciousness. Fortified with this knowledge, we make better life choices and take proactive action to shape our destinies. The intellect growth mindset benefits us individually and fosters a more empathetic and collaborative society where collective growth and development flourish.

Are You Igniting Intellectual Passion for Lifelong Learning?

When the answer to this question is "yes" to passionate engagement, you'll be eager to exchange ideas, knowledge, and learning that fuel your enthusiasm and curiosity. You'll enjoy critical thinking and problem-solving. Afterward, you will be enlightened! When your mind transforms into a thinking apparatus fully immersed in exploring, analyzing, and understanding various subjects, you can transcend formal education. This is a beautiful thing! Individuals who are deeply and passionately engaged tend to showcase a mix of these distinctive traits such as these:

–   **Zeal for Learning:** I just want to learn! An insatiable appetite for learning, driven by a genuine interest in the subject rather than external rewards or obligations.

- **Curiosity:** Really, how does that work? A strong desire to seek knowledge, ask questions, and explore the unknown is a default response. Curiosity serves as the driving force behind their intellectual pursuits.

- **Critical Thinking:** Let's not presume, let's inquire. The ability to analyze information critically, question assumptions, and form well-reasoned opinions based on evidence and logic.

- **Interdisciplinary Exploration:** What links these? A willingness to venture into diverse fields and connect ideas from different domains, recognizing the value of interdisciplinary approaches.

- **Depth of Understanding:** Peel back the onion. A commitment to deeply understanding topics, going beyond surface-level knowledge, and exploring complex nuances.

- **Creativity and Innovation:** Surprise yourself. Integrating knowledge and ideas in novel ways to generate innovative solutions and perspectives.

- **Active Participation:** I'm all in. Engaging in discussions, debates, or intellectual communities to exchange ideas, challenge beliefs, and grow through interactions with others.

- **Personal Growth:** I'm still evolving. Viewing intellectual engagement as a path of personal growth and development, embracing challenges, setbacks, and new insights as opportunities for learning.

- **Appreciation of Diversity:** Viva la difference. Valuing diverse perspectives and respecting the contributions of individuals with different viewpoints and backgrounds.

– **Continuous Pursuit:** On for the long haul. Viewing intellectual engagement as a lifelong journey, recognizing there will always be more to learn and explore.

Overall, passionate intellectual engagement enriches your life by fostering a deeper understanding of the world, encouraging personal growth, and contributing to the greater pool of knowledge and ideas that benefit society as a whole.

***

Great thinkers have historically played a pivotal role in shaping the world and driving significant societal changes. Their passionate engagement is often profound and lasting, influencing multiple dimensions of human existence. I have chosen to highlight women thinkers in diverse fields of expertise and life circumstances, these women exemplify the principles of a growth mindset in their resilience, adaptability, visionary thinking, self-reflection and awareness, commitment to lifelong learning and the courage to challenge the status quo.

• **Innovative Ideas and Concepts:** Great thinkers introduce groundbreaking ideas and concepts that challenge prevailing beliefs and norms. These ideas can revolutionize fields such as science, technology, philosophy, politics, and art, leading to advancements that shape the course of human history. **Dr. Mae Jamison** had the innovative idea of becoming the first African-

American woman to travel to space. In, 1992, she achieved this milestone by joining the crew of the Space Shuttle Endeavour. Her groundbreaking journey shattered barriers, inspiring countless individuals and demonstrating the power of diverse perspectives in the realm of space exploration and beyond.

- **Social and Political Movements**: Many great thinkers have been at the forefront of social and political movements, advocating for equality, justice, and human rights. Their intellectual contributions provide the foundation for social change and inspire collective action toward a more equitable society. An American feminist writer and activist born in 1921, **Bette Friedan** gained prominence with the publication of her groundbreaking book *The Feminine Mystique* in 1963. The book challenged the widely accepted notion that women could find fulfillment only through homemaking and motherhood. Friedan argued that many American women were unhappy in their roles as housewives and experienced a sense of dissatisfaction she termed "the problem that has no name." She co-founded the National Organization for Women (NOW) and authored its vision "...to bring women into the full participation in the mainstream of American society now, exercising all the privileges and responsibilities thereof in truly equal partnership with men."

While met with criticism as more diverse voices emerged within the women's movement for focusing on issues facing primarily white, middle-class, educated, heterosexual woman, she nonetheless remained a visible, ardent, and important advocate for women's rights whom some dubbed the "mother" of the modern women's movement. She was a pivotal figure in changing attitudes, laws, and policies that had limited women's opportunities and rights.

- **Intellectual and Cultural Renaissance:** Great thinkers often lead intellectual and cultural renaissances that ignite a period of significant growth and creativity. These periods of flourishing art, literature, and philosophy propel society forward regarding knowledge, understanding, and appreciation of human achievement. **"The Ninth Street Women"** were a pioneering group of female artists in the mid-20th century who were influential contributors to the Abstract Expressionist movement, which played a significant role in the intellectual and cultural renaissance of that era. Although eleven artists participated in the movement, the book featured five painters. **Grace Hartigan, Joan Mitchell, Helen Frankenthaler, Lee Krasner, and Elaine de Kooning,** were part of this circle that emerged around the vibrant art scene centered around Ninth Street in New York City. These artists were often overshadowed by their male counterparts, such as Jackson Pollock and Willem de Kooning, but their work and ideas were vital in shaping the Abstract Expressionist movement. They broke gender barriers, inspired intellectual exchange, and left a legacy of influence.

- **Scientific Discoveries and Progress:** Through their research and innovative thinking, great scientific minds have made groundbreaking discoveries that revolutionize our understanding of the natural world. These discoveries lead to technological advancements and improvements in various aspects of life. **Marie Curie's** pioneering research on radioactivity led to groundbreaking insights into atomic physics, ultimately transforming our understanding of matter and energy and laying the foundation for modern nuclear science.

- **Educational Impact:** Great thinkers can influence education systems and methodologies, introducing new approaches to learning and fostering critical thinking skills. They may also establish educational institutions that have a long-lasting impact on generations of students. **Marian Wright Edelman**, the founder of the Children's Defense Fund, significantly impacted education through her advocacy for children's rights, equity in education, and access to quality learning opportunities. She believed, "We must not, in trying to think about how we can make a big difference, ignore the small daily differences we can make which over time, add up to big differences that we often cannot foresee."

  Her work has led to policy changes and initiatives that prioritize children's well-being, education, and development, creating a lasting impact on generations of students and underserved communities.

- **Inspiration and Role Models:** Great thinkers serve as role models, inspiring others to pursue intellectual pursuits, think critically, and challenge conventional wisdom. They motivate individuals to contribute positively to society and make a difference in their own fields. **Shelly Lazarus** was known as a prominent figure in the world of advertising and business. She served as the CEO for Ogilvy & Mather, one of the largest and most-well known marketing and advertising agencies in the world, from 1996 to 2008. Lazarus joined the firm in 1971 and worked her way up through the ranks, eventually becoming CEO. Her leadership at the agency was marked by a focus on integrating new digital strategies and traditional advertising methods, as well as fostering a culture of creativity and innovation. Moreover, she was known as a leader who stood up for herself and other women. She considered speaking up not only a part of personal development but part of your job. She is quoted as saying, "Just stand up, do what you need to do, and smile about it."

- **Catalyzing Change in Values and Beliefs:** Through their persuasive arguments and intellectual influence, great thinkers can change societal values and beliefs, shaping ethical frameworks and encouraging compassionate and empathetic behavior. World changer, **Mary McLeod Bethune,** an educator and civil rights leader, was instrumental in transforming societal values and beliefs by advocating for racial and gender equality. Through her leadership in education and her efforts to empower African Americans, she challenged discriminatory norms and laid the groundwork for a more inclusive and just society.

- **Fostering Global Understanding:** Some great thinkers have facilitated cross-cultural understanding and communication by bridging gaps between different communities and promoting international collaboration. **Malala Yousafzai**, an advocate for girls' education and women's rights, has bridged cultures through her courage. Her advocacy through the Malala Fund dedicated to girls education worldwide, her authorship of the memoir *"I Am Malala: The Girl Who Stood Up for Education and Was Shot by the Taliban"*, and her work for the education of refugee girls demonstrate remarkable activism and advocacy efforts.

- **Resolving Complex Problems:** Great thinkers often address complex societal problems by proposing innovative solutions and providing insights that lead to effective problem-solving. **Jane Goodall's** pioneering research on primates transformed our understanding of animal behavior and conservation, leading to innovative solutions for protecting endangered species and ecosystems.

- **Legacy and Enduring Impact:** Their works and ideas continue to have a lasting impact long after they are gone, shaping future generations and contributing to the development of humanity. **Toni Morrison** significantly shaped literature, theater, and language through her profound works and impact on the literary world. As a renowned African-American novelist, her novels, including *Beloved*, *Song of Solomon*, and *The Bluest Eye*, explored complex themes such as identity, race, and history.

Morrison's distinctive narrative style and deep engagement with cultural and social issues have made her a pivotal figure in literature. Her impact extends to theater as well. with works being adapted into powerful stage productions that capture the essence of her storytelling and themes. Moreover, her essays and speeches on language, identity, and literature have contributed to shaping contemporary discussions on these subjects. In terms of language, Morrison's innovative use of language and her exploration of the nuances of communication and expression have inspired generations of writers and readers. Her ability to craft evocative prose and delve into the intricacies of human experience through language has left an indelible mark on literature. Much like Shakespeare, Toni Morrison's literary and cultural influence transcends time and space, enriching literature, theater, and language with her unique voice and perspective.

It is important to note that the impact of great thinkers is not always immediate, and their influence took time and is still being recognized and realized today. Additionally, their contributions are not limited to a particular field but often have interdisciplinary repercussions, leading to a more holistic transformation of the world.

You Have the Power

Malcolm X, the political activist known for his advocacy of Black empowerment, self-reliance, and racial justice, and the love he felt for Black people and their culture said, "Intelligence resides in the skill to adapt across diverse situations, employing knowledge to surmount challenges." The Nation of Islam minister, and other luminaries stand as exemplars of intellect, valor, and resolve, boldly confronting societal norms to instigate transformative change. Their enduring legacies inspire across generations, underscoring the indomitable spirit needed to persist and thrive amid adversity.

Contemplating the mental landscapes of these trailblazers as they grappled with monumental choices gives us a glimpse of their inner realms. Beyond historical accounts, it becomes apparent that their personal journeys entailed a dynamic process encompassing the acquisition, absorption, and application of new insights and aptitudes.

Their intellectual prowess was instrumental in shaping destinies. A foundation of curiosity and receptivity to learning laid the groundwork, coupled with an innate ability to internalize and wield knowledge adeptly, especially when facing watershed decisions that reshaped the world. In their stories, we find a testament to the power of the intellect–the engine that fueled their transformative journeys and left an indelible mark on humanity.

The nurtured intellect is about adopting a growth mindset that empowers us to seek out new challenges, to question the status quo, and be lifelong learners. This mindset not only enriches our own lives but also has the potential to make significant contributions to society at large. Whether it's Sojourner Truth challenging societal norms or Socrates urging us to question our own beliefs, history is replete with examples of individuals who have harnessed their intellect for the greater good. As we move forward, let's carry their legacies with us, continually striving to expand our understanding, challenge our limitations, and to be architects of positive change.

HUSH A MINUTE

Ask yourself… listen to your authentic voice.

What am I curious about?

How can I continuously learn?

How can I apply what I learn?

CHAPTER FIVE

PILLAR #5 SPIRIT

But, as it is written, What no eye has seen, nor ear heard, nor the heart of man imagined, what God has prepared for those who love him, these things God has revealed to us through the Spirit. For the Spirit searches everything, even the depths of God.

(1 Corinthians 2:9-10).

UNVEILING THE DIVINE DEPTHS OF THE SPIRIT: THE FIRE WITHIN

Shortly after retirement from corporate America, I sought the guidance of a life coach and mentor to assist me in charting a path for my new chapter in life. During the intake session she asked, "What do you want to know most?" I was surprised at my rapid response. "I want to know God and make God known." I believe that to be my purpose, and my response reflected it. I was confident in its declaration. I've felt this calling since I realized there is a Being on whom I depend and in whose spirit I abide.

My conviction is innate, layered with a bit of reason and cloaked in universality. I believe in God without needing any proof, and I believe many things about God to be true. The fact that many things about God are a mystery does not negate my innate belief; rather, God's sovereign mystery makes me a humble seeker for truth.

As I deepened my connection with the Spirit, I experienced a heightened awareness of God's presence and an influx of His power into my consciousness. The knowledge I gain from personal experience, teachings, or the results of research and logical reasoning is subordinate to this awareness.

Where reason is applicable, I explain it like this, and I don't presume it to always be logical. For me, God's presence is evident in all we see and experience. On an instinctive level, I believe in God because His presence is stamped on my heart and fulfills my deepest needs.

I am reminded of a famous quote by St. Augustine of Hippo, in his famous passage *Confessions,* in which he states, "You have made us for yourself, O Lord and our heart is restless until it rests in you." The notion of infinite is vague and void until filled with God. I understand myself to be a spiritual being, and, based on that understanding, I believe God is also a spiritual being.

Some theologians may find fault in my assertions because I do not posit facts as if knowledge of God cannot be related to our nature or reasoning process. Others rely almost *solely* on the literalism of Scripture for the basis of their beliefs; "solely" is the operative word. Having been introduced to fundamentalism, I am not opposed to literal hermeneutics; however, I am more concerned with the "seriousness" of Scripture, desiring its message to change me rather than try to change others with my own cultural and traditional biases, which we sometimes risk by solely interpreting the Scriptures literally.

I break down universalism like this: Our minds and bodies have specific abilities and emotions associated with certain things or concepts. For example, our senses rely on the existence of objects they are designed to perceive. Our eyes, for instance, are built in a way that assumes the presence of light. The sense of hearing wouldn't make sense without the concept of sound, and the sense of touch relies on the existence of tangible objects.

Similarly, our social emotions require the existence of relationships suitable for them to be expressed. Likewise, our religious feelings, awareness of dependency, sense of responsibility, desires, and connection to a higher being beyond ourselves and anything in the natural world all point to the existence of God.

The preceding paragraphs lay the foundation for understanding how our innate faculties, experiences, and emotions are connected to the belief in God, the concept of Spirit, and the idea of a growth mindset. This belief stems from the idea that our experiences and internal sense of dependence, responsibility, and fellowship with something greater point to the existence of a divine presence.

A growth mindset captures our innate knowledge and reasoning and suggests that our minds possess inherent capacities and abilities. It highlights that certain knowledge and understanding don't solely come from external sources or experiences but are rooted in our innate constitution. Overall, these ideas weave together by acknowledging our innate faculties, our connection to the divine through our experiences and feelings, and the recognition that our growth and development as individuals involve both our innate capacities and our willingness to cultivate and expand our understanding and abilities.

Sole Purpose is Soul Purpose

Acknowledging the existence of a higher being or divine power can provide a framework for understanding that there is a greater purpose to our lives and that our personal growth and development are part of a larger plan. This belief can inspire us to embrace challenges, learn from setbacks, and persist in our efforts to reach our full potential.

This understanding becomes more than just a concept for me; it becomes tangible and transformative. I not only believe in the Spirit but also embody it, allowing it to guide and empower me in fulfilling my purpose. The Spirit takes on various roles in my life.

As a **counselor,** the Spirit offers guidance, insights, and clarity in moments of confusion or decision-making. The Spirit provides me with the wisdom and discernment to navigate life's challenges and make choices aligned with my purpose. The Spirit can do the same for you. Having this counselor is like having round-the-clock access to a therapist who customizes their approach, taking into account our individual experiences, emotions, and aspirations. We are never alone.

As a constant **companion,** the Spirit offers comfort, solace, and support in times of joy, sorrow, or loneliness. We can be assured of a divine presence, reminding us that we have a source of strength and comfort by our side.

I vividly recall the moment when I faced the unexpected death of my father. My family and I were on our way to surprise him for Father's Day in June 2005. However, circumstances swiftly changed. While we were en route to Dayton, my cousin called to inform me my dad had checked himself into the VA hospital due to breathing difficulties. It more serious than anyone knew. Sadly, he passed away before we could reach him. I had no prior knowledge of his illness or its duration. I was completely taken aback.

Despite the shock and grief, I found a profound sense of peace and confidence deep within my soul. It was as if God's presence, carried by His spirit, enveloped me, enabling me to navigate the challenging circumstances that lay ahead. I remember one particular morning, standing alone in the backyard of my father's house where I used to watch him and his friends engage in the sport of racoon trapping. *Coon* trapping had its own kind of spectacle. In that solitary moment, amidst the quiet yard, I could faintly hear the echoes of my dad's laughter. I couldn't help but utter the words, "God Is," over and over. It was a simple yet powerful affirmation of God's unwavering existence and a testament to the faith that anchored me. With this newfound strength, I gathered myself and returned to the hotel, ready to face whatever came. I sat in our room at the hotel desk, retrieved my laptop, and wrote:

A Father's Day Surprise

Rather than send a greeting card to my dad this year for Father's Day, my family and I thought it would be a special treat if we trekked the 400+ miles to appear unexpectedly at his door on Sunday, June 19, 2005. However, our sovereign God had other plans. He wanted John to spend this Father's Day with Him. For as much as we love my dad, God loves him more; thus, He decided that it was time for John to make his trip home. So, I sit here, choked with grief on this Father's Day, however, comforted, knowing that my dad is in the arms of God.

Resolved, I continued to write, telling stories and thanking family and friends for their loyalty and presence. How was I able to do this? The tangible Spirit of God carried me.

The Spirit is a ***comforter.*** In moments of distress or pain, the Spirit acts as a comforter, bringing peace, healing, and reassurance to our souls. The Spirit provides solace and a sense of divine embrace, enveloping us with unconditional love and a profound understanding of our needs. Sometimes in these moments, one doesn't know what is needed. We can be assured that the Spirit knows and understands what we need when we need it.

The Spirit also serves as a ***connector,*** deepening our connection with God and others. It fosters a sense of unity, love, and compassion, enabling us to forge meaningful relationships and extend kindness and understanding to those around us. It encourages a sense of oneness with humanity and all creation. Think about that the next time you buy a meal for a homeless person, pay the bill at Starbucks for the patron behind you, are the peacemaker in a family dispute, or pray or say a kind word for someone. You are making a spiritual connection.

The Spirit is a ***course corrector.*** The Spirit functions as a course corrector, gently nudging us back on track when we veer off the intended path. It helps us realign with our purpose, guiding us toward growth, transformation, and fulfilling our true potential. I love it when the Spirit helps me learn from my mistakes, make necessary adjustments, and continue progressing.

By embracing and leveraging the Spirit in these roles, I have experienced a profound transformation in my life. It becomes more than a mere belief; it becomes an active force that shapes my thoughts, actions, and interactions. Through the Spirit's guidance and influence, I find strength, purpose, and fulfillment as I navigate the complexities of life, and so can you.

Spirit is our Super Power

As spiritual beings, we tap into a deeper part of ourselves that transcends the physical world's limitations. I liken it to a superpower, not in the *Marvel* sense, but in a supernatural sense, whereby we invite or invoke power into our souls from our Creator. We often forget that power is available because we operate so much in our humanness. However, understanding our spiritual essence can empower us to cultivate qualities such as resilience, compassion, and gratitude, which are integral to a growth mindset.

By connecting with our spirit, we can draw upon inner resources to overcome obstacles, foster personal growth, and embrace continuous learning and improvement. We are spirit beings clothed in bodies; our physical realm extends into the spiritual realm. From the perspective of a growth mindset, this suggests that there is more to our existence than what is purely physical or material.

Knowing and embracing this mindset emphasizes nurturing your spiritual well-being, exploring your inner essence, and seeking a connection with the divine aspect of existence. Thinking in these terms makes a growth mindset tangible. The relationship between God, Spirit, and a growth mindset lies in the interconnectedness of purpose, unlimited potential, inner strength, and the continuous pursuit of personal growth. By recognizing our spiritual nature, embracing a belief in a higher power, and adopting a growth mindset, we can find inspiration, resilience, and the motivation to cultivate our abilities, embrace learning, and strive for personal and spiritual development. God's Spirit provides access to the divine.

The Spirit is my sacred channel for connecting with God and experiencing His love. By doing so, I can become the highest version of myself and fulfill my purpose on this planet. The power of our spirit is integral to fulfilling our purpose in life. When we establish a deep connection with the Spirit, we experience love and gain a clearer understanding and appreciation of God's plan for our individual journeys.

Soul Sanctuary

"Within you, there is a stillness and a sanctuary to which you can retreat at any time and be yourself."

- Herman Hesse

With its profound essence, the Spirit is often likened to a wellspring of boundless wisdom and unwavering strength, a divine presence within us, serving as a bridge that connects us to the limitless source of wisdom and power that emanates from God. To tap into the Spirit is to unlock the floodgates of guidance, insight, and empowerment that reside within. Let your soul become a sanctuary, a sacred abode for the divine to dwell.

Our soul sanctuary is the place to nurture a deep and personal relationship with God, cultivating a bond that transcends the ordinary. When we fully embrace and surrender to the divine flow, a concept challenging to put into words, but akin to experiencing serendipity fueled by the guiding hand of the Spirit. It's like suddenly finding all the lanes open on a once congested highway, where obstacles dissolve, and we experience a smooth, effortless journey. It's when abstract concepts become crystal clear just as we need them for an important exam, when deals effortlessly close, meetings align perfectly with our schedule, and we discover that the item we're about to purchase is unexpectedly on sale when the cashier rings it up.

It's as if the Spirit hovers over our circumstances, orchestrating them like the gentle flow of a river, leading us seamlessly to our desired destination or fulfilling our essential needs. In these moments, we sense a harmonious alignment with the universe, where everything falls into place with an almost magical ease.

Serendipity is what it can feel like when we embark on a journey that allows us to explore the profound depths of our authentic selves. Within the boundless realm of the Spirit, we find tangible keys that unlock our truest potential, revealing concrete pathways to self-discovery and growth. In this sacred space, intimacy flourishes, and your connection to the wellspring becomes a vibrant current, infusing every aspect of your being.

To fully unlock your potential, requires letting go of self-imposed limitations, fears, and resistance. By surrendering, you allow the divine energy to guide and shape your path. It is in this surrender that you truly discover the depths of your authentic self, your true identity that is aligned with your divine essence. Consider embracing your true self, tapping into the Spirit within.

The Spirit pillar explores the profound connection between spirit and soul in a growth mindset, emphasizing that to abide in the spirit is to find one's true purpose. It posits that your soul's purpose is, in essence, your sole purpose in life. The spirit serves as a powerful engine for this journey. We get in touch with our spirit in our soul's sanctuary, a sacred space within where we recharge, reflect, and reconnect with our innermost selves.

HUSH A MINUTE

Ask yourself… and listen in your authentic voice.

What specific scriptures or spiritual teachings resonate most with my belief and values?

Which spiritual discipline, such as meditation, journaling, or self-reflection, do I feel drawn to explore further to foster the work of the Spirit within me?

When faced with significant challenges, decisions, or uncertainties, how do I currently seek guidance and surrender my will to divine wisdom?

AFTERWORD

Can you feel the anticipation in the air? It's palpable. There is an undeniable space in this vast world, eagerly waiting to embrace your uniqueness, gifts, talents, dreams, skills, kindness, and intellect. All of it!

I am thrilled that we've met on this journey. My excitement bubbles over. I deeply cherish this moment, as I have the privilege to speak words of life to you. You bring a radiant light that the world yearns for, and we are eagerly waiting for you to cast away your hiding place and unleash the full power of your boundless potential. It fills my heart with joy to imagine the incredible impact you will make once you step into your authentic self.

You possess a tapestry of qualities and abilities that no one else can replicate. Embrace the truth that no one is quite like you, a gift beyond measure. The world hungers for your presence, contributions, and the unique perspectives only you can offer.

Let this be when you shed the invisibility cloak and allow your brilliance to shine. Embrace the growth mindset that resides within you. Honor your dreams and aspirations, for they hold the keys to unlocking a life of fulfillment and purpose. Believe in your worth, and let your passions fuel your journey.

No longer should you hold back or dim your light. It's time to take center stage and reveal your true self. Embrace your inherent power, unleash your potential, and let your vibrant spirit radiate far and wide. We eagerly await the moment you step into your greatness and share the extraordinary gifts you possess.

***

One of my guilty pleasures is binge-watching the period drama *Bridgerton*. In it, Lady Danbury, a widow and one of the most prominent figures in the regency drama, is the self-appointed "guardian" and maternal figure for the son of her close friend the Duchess of Hastings. As an infant, the child became the in-line successor to the Duke of Hastings. As a young boy, he suffered from a speech impediment, which his father considered an embarrassment. He ordered the child's governess to keep the young boy hidden until he was sent away to boarding school. The heir's existence had all but been forgotten in English Ton.

Although he had mastered most regency leadership expectations for a royal heir—he was expertly tutored, and exceptionally literate, skilled in horsemanship, and fencing—he remained in the shadows until the dowager took interest in him. Lady Danbury recognized his potential and agreed to help him overcome his stutter. "You can speak," she declared. In exchange for her sponsorship, she demanded, 'when you enter the room, be worthy of the attention you command."

Well, I'm *your* lady, sister, girlfriend, and person, and writing to tell you that you are worthy, exceptional, skilled, and beautiful; you have the power, and *you* are enough. *you can speak-* life into your mind, body, and soul. It is time for you to step into the light so the world can see you and bask in your brilliance.

Remember, you are not alone on this journey. Countless souls are cheering you on, supporting you, and ready to witness the magic you will create. So, my dear, it's time to let go of hiding, step forward, and claim your rightful place. The world is ready, waiting with open arms, to celebrate the awe-inspiring force that is you.

Remember this! There is no one else like you! Embrace your unique journey, your strengths, and your potential. Each step you take toward growth and empowerment is a testament to your remarkable spirit. As you champion your growth mindset, I'm here to cheer you on. Your efforts to unlock your potential and embrace the pillars of belief, self-insight, spirit, intellect, and abilities are truly inspiring. Keep pushing forward, keep embracing challenges, and keep believing in yourself. You are truth in the making, and so it is here that we end this book to begin anew!

Xoxo

Lady Jocelyn:-)

Fun fact: It turns out that I have Scottish and Nigerian ancestry in my DNA. My daughter bought a souvenir plot of land in Scotland's Highland Titles Nature Reserve. I have been granted the title Lady Jocelyn Lee, Lady of Glencoe. It's official! Your lady is honored to meet you; however, the best honor is to call me friend.

SOURCES

My research is grounded in a diverse array of sources including books, articles, films, private archival materials, biblical commentaries, and firsthand accounts.

Efforts have been made to accurately and comprehensively attribute credit to original authors and creators.

Any omissions or inaccuracies in citations are unintentional. All requisite citations have been documented.

Chittister, J. (2022). An evolving God, an evolving purpose, an evolving world. London, Fortress Press.

Dweck, C. S. (2006). *Mindset: The new psychology of success.* New York, Ballantine Books.

Grant, A. (2021). *Think again.* New York, Viking.

Holiday, R. (2014). *The obstacle is the way.* New York, Penguin.

Johanssen, M. (2023). *Growth Mindset: The unstoppable you.* Las Vegas. [Place of publication not identified].

Pipher, M. (2006). *Writing to change the world.* New York, Penguin Group.

Rohr, R. (2011). *Wonderous encounters: Scripture for Lent.* Cincinnati, Franciscan Media.

ACKNOWLEDGMENTS

I am an only child but I've never felt alone. There has always been someone in my life supporting me, encouraging me, and laboring with me through countless starts and stops to becoming.

From cheerleaders to raving fans, tough critics to comforters, purveyors of possibilities to prayer partners; with deep humility, profound gratitude, and overwhelming joy, I wholeheartedly express my heartfelt appreciation to the following:

My HUSBAND, Myron, for relentlessly fueling the fire of my dreams, and for your unwavering devotion, and resolute support that knows no bounds. You are my fierce and meticulous in-house editor, tirelessly scrutinizing every word. You see the potential in me even when I doubt myself, and for that, I am forever indebted to you. I love you with a passion that burns brighter than a thousand suns.

My PARENTS, Ethel, and John (Posthumously). Dad, with a profound appreciation for your love and affirmation. Your creative spirit and infectious sense of humor have become an intrinsic part of who I am today, and for that, I am eternally grateful.

Mom, thank you for endowing me with strength and resilience. Your unconditional love and the way it manifests in my life are truly invaluable. My heart swells with immense gratitude as I express my deepest appreciation to you. You have been the catalyst, the very source of my literary journey, and for that, I am forever indebted to you. From the time you placed my very first book, the ABC Book for Babies in my chubby hands, I devoured its contents (literally), the actual words themselves. I gnawed on those precious pages, ingesting the letters that would later become the foundation of my love for reading and writing. As I grew older and my literary appetite intensified, you went above and beyond to nurture my passion. You ingeniously crafted books for me out of construction paper and carefully collected pages from the Milwaukee Green Sheet. With each homemade creation, you fueled my imagination and instilled in me a profound appreciation for the written word. Those humble creations were not merely books but gateways to new worlds, windows into endless possibilities. And for that, I will forever cherish you and the immeasurable impact you have had on my life.

Our CHILDREN, Rebekah, for teaching me how to love purely and for being my mirror into self-insight, and sons, Marvelle and Marques, for your trust as I learned how to parent, and for showing me grace when I didn't always get it right.

My BESTIES, Regina and Victoria, you have been unwavering pillars in my life. I hold you close to my heart with deep appreciation and boundless affection.

My SISTER FRIENDS, Carla, Kathy, Patti, Sophia, and Wanda, for *"getting me,"* and loving me anyway. You all are like a sumptuous recipe for life's ebbs and flows.

My EDITOR, Kim Suhr, who has not only polished my writing with her careful touch but has also nurtured my craft, especially during the critical moments when I began to take writing seriously.

My TEAM Jason Heras, Yolanda Lake, and Dana Gibbons for your professionalism, artistic talents, and care when curating the composite elements to present me and my work to the world.

My EARLY READERS Deborah Harris, Kathy Scott, and Dr. Marcelle Haddix, for helping to refine and enhance the book's message. I am incredibly grateful for your labor of love.

My incredible COACHES and MENTORS, Pamela Lue-Hing, and Dr. Lea Williams, who have selflessly guided me, offering unwavering support, and holding my hand through each significant milestone. I am blessed with your enduring friendship.

The countless teachers, students, pastors, and colleagues, who have consistently uplifted and motivated me to translate my thoughts into written words.

It goes without saying, to each and every one of you who reads this book, your curiosity and open-mindedness are the keys that unlock your own potential, fostering the growth mindset that propels us all toward a fulfilled life and toward greater heights.

Finally, to the matchless glory of almighty GOD.

APPENDIX

GROWTH MINDSET
TOOLKIT

PILLAR #1: BELIEF

Get Unstuck

Belief thrives when you surround yourself with supportive and like-minded individuals who encourage and inspire you. Sharing your aspirations and dreams with others who believe in you can further reinforce our own beliefs and motivate you to act.

As such, you must remove what no longer serves you. When you do, the right opportunities and people will find you when your purpose and energy are aligned. The meaning of "avoiding people and things that no longer serve you" is rooted in the pursuit of personal growth and the quest to break free from stagnation. It involves recognizing that certain individuals, relationships, and circumstances may hinder your progress, drain your energy, and consciously detach you from yourself.

To truly get unstuck and propel yourself forward, you must have courage. This could involve distancing yourself from toxic relationships, negative influences, self-limiting beliefs, or unproductive habits. You create space for new opportunities, positive influences, and personal transformation by releasing the anchors that hold you back.

Getting unstuck requires you to evaluate your surroundings and relationships discerningly. It involves reflecting on whether the people and things in your life contribute positively to your growth, supports your aspirations, and align with your values. It also necessitates self-reflection to identify internal factors, such as limiting beliefs or negative self-talk, that may hold you captive.

Try this:

Take a moment to assess your relationships and connections, both personal and professional.

Consider whether it is time to distance yourself from individuals who bring negative energy or hold you back from reaching your potential.

Identify and explore ways to release these areas, making space for new beliefs and empowering habits.

Once you've identified what no longer serves you. It's essential to actively seek out positive influences and experiences that align with your aspirations.

Surround yourself with individuals who uplift, inspire and encourage personal growth. Seek opportunities like mentorship or learning experiences that expand your horizon and challenge you to evolve. By honestly confronting and letting go of what no longer serves you, you can free ourselves from stagnation and create a path toward growth and fulfillment. Embracing this concept empowers you to consciously curate your environments, relationships, and beliefs, paving the way for personal transformation and unlocking our potential.

Maintain Positive Thoughts and Speak Positive Words

Instead of focusing solely on finding your purpose, consider releasing the weights holding you back. When you do so, your purpose will naturally emerge, and you can live a more fulfilling and authentic life. The presence of doubt, insecurity, and fear can lead to the opening of old wounds, sabotaging your dreams and goals; however, being able to harness belief does not mean you will never *doubt*, but whenever you catch yourself thinking negative thoughts, cancel them! Your belief will anchor you, and you will accomplish what you set out to do.

Sending positive thoughts into the universe emphasizes the power of your words and intentions in shaping your reality. It suggests that by consciously expressing positive thoughts, affirmations, and intentions, you can attract positivity, abundance, and opportunities into our lives. When you speak positive thoughts into the universe, you tap into the principles of manifestation and the law of attraction. By aligning your words and thoughts with what you desire, you create a vibrational frequency that resonates with those desires. This alignment catalyzes bringing them into existence.

Your words hold immense creative power. They not only impact our mindset and beliefs but also send energetic ripples out into the world. By consciously choosing positive and uplifting words, you cultivate an environment that supports growth, nurtures well-being, and attracts positive experiences. Speaking positive thoughts into the universe requires mindfulness and intentionality. It involves reprogramming your internal dialogue, replacing self-doubt and negative self-talk with affirmations and empowering statements. By consistently expressing positive thoughts, you shape your perception, reinforce your beliefs, and ultimately manifest your desired reality.

Try this:

Reflect on your current self-talk and identify any negativity or self-limiting language patterns.

Commit to replacing those negative thoughts with positive affirmations and empowering statements.

Recognize the impact you have on others.

Consciously choose to speak words of encouragement, support, and kindness.

Remember this is for you and to cultivate an atmosphere of positivity around you to attract other like-minded individuals.

Take a moment to reflect on your deepest desires and intentions.

Consider how you can translate those desires into positive, present-tense affirmations or statements.

Be intentional about aligning your spoken words with your authentic self and the life you want to create.

Regularly revisit your intentions and affirm them through conscious and positive self-expression.

Practice Gratitude

Practicing gratitude emphasizes the transformative power of acknowledging and appreciating the blessings, experiences, and people in our lives. It involves cultivating a mindset of gratitude, in which you intentionally shift your focus to recognize the positive aspects of existence, even amidst challenges or adversity.

When you practice gratitude, you align yourself with a growth mindset. By embracing gratitude, you develop a lens through which you can perceive these opportunities more clearly, fostering resilience, optimism, and a sense of abundance.

Gratitude opens your heart and mind to the present moment, allowing you to savor the joys and find meaning in the simplest things. It shifts your perspective from scarcity to abundance, from focusing on what is lacking to appreciating what you have. This shift in mindset empowers you to approach challenges with a sense of resilience and optimism as you recognize the potential for growth and learning within every situation.

Try this:

Consider implementing a dedicated practice or expressing gratitude on a daily basis.

Keep a gratitude journal, where you write down three things you are grateful for daily.

Upon waking and before your feet hit the floor, thank God that your body is moving and your senses are. Take a moment during your morning routine to meditate in thankfulness.

Reflect on how you can cultivate gratitude even in the face of adversity.

Consider how hardships can offer lessons, growth opportunities, or a chance to appreciate the strength and resilience within yourself.

Practice being thankful even in the midst of difficulty. (Your emotions may not line up with this one, but do it anyway). Your attitude will change you, even if the circumstances don't shift right away!

Acknowledge, appreciate, express, and support acts of kindness in their presence. (This may seem uncomfortable at first, but the more you do, it gets easier and is more authentic.)

Consider how you can have heartfelt conversations, small gestures, or written notes/texts of appreciation.

Sometimes when you can't find the words to say what you want, do something instead like bringing a coffee from your local coffee shop, picking up some flowers at the grocery store, or pulling the trash cart in from the night before. It's the little things that add up. Pray and ask God, "What does my friend or neighbor need that I can help with?"

By embracing the challenge of practicing gratitude, you invite profound shifts in your mindset and perspective. Cultivating gratitude enhances your well-being and joy, and fuels your growth, resilience, and ability to navigate life's challenges gracefully. Let gratitude guide your perception, relationships, and personal growth, leading you to a life filled with abundant blessings and fulfillment.

Embrace Your Funny Side: Are You Up to the Challenge?

1. Gratitude Practice Challenge: Can you handle *The Thankful Three?* Grab your gratitude journal daily and write three things you're grateful for. Whether it's your pet's hilarious antics, a perfectly brewed cup of coffee, or your bed's soft embrace, unleash your gratitude superpowers and conquer this quest of appreciation! I often do this at the end of the day and close my eyes with joyful, grateful thoughts.

2. Finding Gratitude in Tough Times: Your mission, should you accept it, is to uncover the hidden gems in challenging situations. Can you spot the silver lining amidst a flat tire, a rainy day, or a failed recipe? Get your gratitude magnifying glass ready, detective, and let's solve the case of the sneaky blessings! Okay, sometimes it's like this! Some days it is hard to think of sneaky blessings, but when you look at it this way, you *will* find something to be thankful for.

3. Expressing Gratitude Galore: Are you prepared for the Gratitude Extravaganza? Get ready to spread gratitude like confetti! Challenge yourself to surprise at least three people each week with heartfelt expressions of appreciation. Whether it's a spontaneous dance of gratitude or a silly thank-you note, unleash your inner gratitude superhero and make the world a brighter place, one grateful moment at a time!

Remember, the essence of these funny challenge questions is to bring joy and lightheartedness to the practice of gratitude. Embrace the laughter, have fun with it, and let gratitude become a playful and uplifting part of your life's journey!

Memorialize in a Journal

I believe it is essential to write down what you learn. My journaling isn't faithful, meaning I don't write daily. However, I journal to remember key events, insights, and experiences that have changed my life. I document them for recall during challenging times. I lay stones to memorialize events, as Joshua and the twelve tribes did when they crossed the Jordan. To summon your belief, lay some stones. Start a journal today!

Keeping a journal enables you to deepen your self-awareness, gain insights into your thoughts and emotions, and track your progress over time. It provides a safe space for self-expression, allowing you to explore your dreams, fears, and aspirations. Through the act of writing, you engage in a process of introspection and self-discovery, nurturing our personal growth journey.

Journaling aligns seamlessly with a growth mindset, encouraging you to embrace challenges, seek learning opportunities, and reflect on your experiences. By documenting your achievements, setbacks, and lessons learned, you gain valuable perspectives contributing to our ongoing growth and development.

As I mentioned, I use several methods to journal. *Notes* and also *Day One* are my go-to apps on my iPhone. Both are convenient and easy to use. At the time of printing there are other online apps that could be useful based on the functions you appreciate.

Day One: A popular journaling app with a user-friendly interface, customizable features, and the option to add photos and locations. You can even add photos.

Journey: An app that focuses on journaling and self-reflection, offering prompts, mood tracking, and the ability to attach images and audio.

Penzu: A secure and private journaling app that allows you to customize entries, add photos, and sync across devices.

Diaro: A versatile journaling app with password protection, cloud sync, and the ability to add tags and organize entries.

Allow your journal to be a trusted companion, guiding you through the ups and downs of life and serving as a testament to your growth and evolution.

PILLAR #2: ABILITIES

Being gifted with abilities yet unrecognized is a discouraging experience. Just as my early teacher's admonishment shook my confidence, such instances have the potential to sow doubt and overshadow the very talents that define us. As someone who has traveled extensively by airplane, I remember pilot maneuvers during turbulence. I introduce them here as a metaphor to deal with the predicament of unrecognized talent.

Try this:

Adjust Your Perspective

Like a plane navigating through turbulence, when abilities go unnoticed, it's like flying blind without adjusting your altitude. Returning to recalibrate your perspective can unveil hidden dimensions of your capabilities. This shift in viewpoint can illuminate alternative approaches to challenges, unveiling solutions previously concealed by self-doubt.

Rely on Guidance

Imagine this journey as tuning in to your radar. A radar's capacity to detect what's beyond the immediate view resides within, awaiting your acknowledgment. Tapping into this intuitive guidance system fosters emotional intelligence, enabling a profound understanding of both yourself and others.

This invaluable insight enhances decision-making and amplifies problem-solving prowess.

In those moments when unrecognized abilities cast shadows, a third pilot maneuver comes into play.

Pivot with Grace

Much like an aircraft's graceful turn, you must pivot with gentleness and compassion. Showcasing resilience while responding to unforeseen challenges fosters a sense of calm, echoing your wisdom about practicing self-compassion. Just as a pilot navigates changing conditions, you navigate the uncertainties of life, embracing kindness as a cornerstone for sound decision-making and emotional well-being.

Try this:

Explore Your Abilities

Intellectual Abilities: Harness your cognitive prowess by honing critical thinking, memory, logical reasoning, and problem-solving skills. Engage in mental exercises and tasks that promote intellectual growth.

Physical Abilities: Nourish your physical well-being by nurturing motor skills, coordination, strength, and agility. Whether it's sports, arts, or labor, focus on activities that amplify your physical capabilities.

Creative Abilities: Unleash your imagination and innovation. Cultivate artistic expression, lateral thinking, unconventional problem-solving, and the art of generating original ideas.

Social and Emotional Abilities: Foster your skills in connecting with others. Enhance your communication, empathy, emotional intelligence, and self-awareness. These abilities empower you to navigate and forge meaningful relationships.

Identify Your Abilities: What are your innate, strengths and talents? List as many as you can: intellectual, physical, creative, social, and emotional. Consider traits that others have told you that you have as well as those that are apparent to you.

Prioritize with Purpose: Which of your abilities are most important? How do they align with your personal and professional goals?

Develop actionable steps: How can you put these abilities to work for you in your structured plan for growth? For example, for my health and well- being I will meditate starting with 12 minutes a day until I reach 60 minutes in 30 days. I will also start intermittent fasting beginning with 12 hours a week, and increase an hour every week until I reach 16 hours in total every day.

Embrace Lifelong Learning: Delve into resources that deepen your understanding of your abilities.

Explore books, articles, videos, and online courses to gain new insights.

PILLAR # 3 SELF-INSIGHT

Try this:

Embrace the Power of Self-Awareness: Cultivate a heightened awareness in the present moment. Pay attention to your thoughts, emotions, and behaviors, recognizing how they shape your interactions and choices. Being attuned to your internal world and external reactions will deepen your understanding of yourself.

Harness Emotional Intelligence: Explore the depths of your emotional landscape, understanding and managing your emotions gracefully. Pay attention to patterns and triggers, developing the ability to navigate your emotions in ways that positively impact yourself and those around you. Emotional intelligence will empower you to forge deeper connections and foster personal growth.

Seek Feedback and Assess Yourself: Embrace the wisdom of others by actively seeking feedback and guidance. Engage in conversations offering different perspectives and open yourself to constructive criticism. By integrating feedback and honestly assessing your performance and behaviors, you'll gain valuable insights and uncover areas for growth.

Embrace a Growth Mindset: Be open to challenging assumptions, beliefs, and behaviors that no longer serve you. Cultivate a mindset that thrives on learning and embraces change. Embrace the journey of growth, constantly evolving and expanding your self-insight along the way.

PILLAR #4 INTELLECT

KEEP YOUR MIND OPEN TO OTHER DISCIPLINES

Avoid confining yourself to a single discipline; instead, embrace a wide variety of fields and subjects. By exploring various areas of knowledge, you enrich your understanding, nurture creativity, and foster a broader perspective that can lead to innovative insights and holistic problem-solving.

Try this:

EVOLVE

Evolve to a New Era encapsulates a transformative journey propelled by the intellectual growth mindset, guiding us from familiar landscapes into uncharted territories of advancement and enlightenment. This concept signifies an epoch where the thirst for knowledge, empathy, and collaboration serve as the compass for humanity's progression.

Pursuing truth becomes a shared endeavor, where the accumulation of wisdom is cherished as an invaluable asset. Empathy and humility are pillars of your intellectual voyage as you navigate this uncharted territory. Empathy enables you to understand the diverse perspectives of fellow travelers on this journey, fostering a compassionate understanding of the challenges and triumphs they face. Humility asserts that no single mind possesses all the answers; every individual's unique growth journey contributes to the tapestry of collective advancement.

KEEP UP!

Don't allow your knowledge to become stale. The pursuit of knowledge is an ongoing voyage requiring constant renewal and expansion. Just as a pool stagnates without fresh water, your intellect can wither if you cease to challenge yourself. In a world that evolves at an unprecedented pace, clinging to outdated or static knowledge can lead to missed opportunities and a narrowing of perspectives.

In a practical sense, avoiding intellectual stagnation demands an appetite for exploration. You must venture beyond your comfort zones and engage with topics that might initially seem unfamiliar or uncomfortable. It invites you to question assumptions, challenge long-held beliefs, and accept that our current knowledge is just a snapshot in the grand mosaic of human understanding. Best-selling author, Adam Grant challenges his audience to make a long list of the things of which they are ignorant—he lists approximately eight areas.

I have made a list of twelve areas to explore one for every month of the year:

resources for caregivers

environmental sustainability

my Scottish and Nigerian ancestry

astronomy

quantum physics-energy

technology like AI

local legislation and politics

mental health

expatriation

gardening in Arizona

change writing in fiction

training my Labrador Retriever, Solomon (he is a new breed for our family- and ooh, what we don't know!)

Through generating your own list, you will unlock the potential for lifelong learning, dynamic adaptability, and a profound sense of growth. Join me, won't you?

STAY IN THE QUESTION

Being an intellectual is about having the courage to ask questions and look for answers even when the result may be uncomfortable. To achieve this, you must have the freedom to think critically and the ability to look at things from different angles. It is the ability to use knowledge effectively and creatively. It is about using the tools at your disposal to identify, understand, and solve problems. It involves challenging our preconceptions and scrutinizing your biases.

Some beliefs are so ingrained that you don't even realize you're clinging to outdated viewpoints instead of grappling with new ones. Avoid falling into the trap of "mental miserliness," a term scientists use to describe cognitive complacency. You can always increase your intelligence. Acquaint yourself with people who think differently than you. You won't agree on everything, but you will find the wisdom in a different ideology.

By embracing an intellectual growth mindset, you transcend the confines of limited thinking and open yourself to boundless possibilities. This mindset will empower you to think both broadly and boldly, breaking free from the shackles of self-imposed limitations. As you nurture this growth-oriented perspective, you give birth to your own intellectual evolution and expanded consciousness.

Reasoning and Logic: My journey into mastering reasoning and logic took shape during my graduate studies in religion. With a deep devotion to understanding the Bible, I embarked on a quest to systematically approach and interpret Scripture, embracing the method of exegesis – a structured approach that hinges on reason and logic. Through this disciplined process, the layers of meaning within religious texts unfold, revealing insights that are integral to comprehending ancient wisdom.

The practice involves wielding logical thinking to forge connections, draw evidence-backed conclusions, and navigate the intricate tapestry of interpretations. Because I love reading Scripture I didn't want to be left at the mercy of my own cultural background, limited education, and in particular my own biases. My engagement encompassed contextual analysis, textual scrutiny, comparative exploration, and historical and cultural interpretation, forging a path toward pattern recognition and insightful understanding. With each endeavor, this form of thinking solidified into an inherent part of my intellectual toolkit.

Critical Thinking: My academic journey provided the perfect arena for nurturing this skill. Interestingly, the absence of structured learning, later on, made me acutely aware of the risk of mental stagnation. In response, I consciously engaged in questioning assumptions, embracing multiple perspectives, dissecting media narratives for biases, and dedicating time to evaluate my own thought processes. This commitment to ongoing mental acuity has evolved into a personal ethos, constantly propelling me to perceive the layers beneath the surface.

Question to Ponder: What are three things you can do in the next week to sharpen your critical thinking skills?

Problem-Solving: The art of problem-solving, a skill I honed through various professional roles, involves identifying issues, devising innovative solutions, and effectively implementing them. Logic and reason are the compass in this endeavor, steering the exploration of alternative viewpoints and adapting strategies. My experiences, especially when engaging with senior managers, underscored the significance of not just presenting ideas but also backing them up with feasible solutions.

Intellectual Curiosity and Exploration: The allure of intellectual curiosity and exploration fuels my desire to embrace new ideas, knowledge, and experiences. This innate urge compels me to ask questions, delve into diverse subjects, and pursue a lifelong quest for learning.

⬛ PILLAR #5 SPIRIT ⬛

Try this:

Seek to understand and apply God's word. Engage with scripture and spiritual teachings that align with your beliefs. Regularly study and meditate on God's word, seeking to understand His principles. As you deepen your knowledge and understanding strive to apply these teachings daily.

Embrace spiritual disciplines. Engage in spiritual disciplines that foster the work of the Spirit within you. This can include practices such as meditation, journaling, and self-reflection. Set aside a regular time to be still and listen to the whispers of the Spirit. As you cultivate a deeper awareness of the Spirit's presence, you open yourself up to its transformative power, allowing it to shape your character and refine your values.

Seek guidance and surrender. Regularly seek guidance from the Spirit and surrender your will to divine wisdom. Whenever faced with challenges or decisions or uncertainties, pause and seek the Spirit's guidance through prayer and or quiet contemplation. Ask for clarity, discernment, and strength. Trust the Spirit's leading and surrender your desires and plans to God's higher purpose. By surrendering and relying on the Spirit's guidance, you equip yourself with the tools necessary to navigate life's challenges with grace and resilience.

Spend time in nature. Nature can help us to connect with the Spirit. Spending time in nature can lead us to calm and peace as we focus on the beauty of our surroundings and the Spirit. My favorite time of the morning is early daybreak. I finish waking up on my patio and I am especially attuned to the singing birds, and skuttle of geckos and lizards. They appear to play with abandon. As the steam escapes from my coffee to dance in the breeze, my eyes follow it upward to the sky where the clouds drift along seeming to touch the peaks of the mountains. I am immersed in nature and my cheeks become moist as tears stream down my face. God is present in nature and I meet Him there.

Listen and discern. Actively listen and discern the guidance of the Spirit. Pay attention to the subtle nudges, intuitive feelings, and inner promptings that arise within you. Be receptive and open to receiving messages from the Spirit. Be aware that sometimes the guidance may come as a deep sense of knowing, a gentle conviction, or a profound peace. Trust your intuition and discern what aligns with the wisdom and values of the divine presence within you.

Live in alignment. Strive to live in alignment with the teachings and principles of the Spirit. Engage in practices that nurture your spiritual growth, such as studying sacred texts, engaging in acts of compassion and service, and cultivating virtues such as love, kindness, and forgiveness. By aligning your thoughts, words, and actions with the divine wisdom, you create a harmonious resonance with the Spirit, allow it to flow freely, and infuse you with its strength and guidance.

Live in awe of God, experiencing gratitude and adoration. Praise is an expression of gratitude and adoration towards God. When you offer heartfelt praise, you acknowledge God's shifting the spiritual atmosphere. Certain melodies, harmonies, and lyrics can stir our spirits and create an environment conducive to encountering the supernatural. Music has the ability to uplift, inspire, and connect us with the transcendent By incorporating worship music and songs of praise, you set the stage for a spiritual atmosphere where miracles, healing, and diving encounters can occur.

SPIRIT IS YOUR SUPERPOWER

You are more than you realize!

1. I believe in a dualistic nature, both a physical aspect and spiritual; the spiritual aspect being your essence or soul. This implies you are not limited. *You are more!*

2. I believe humans have a spiritual identity, a spiritual dimension where their core identity is rooted in the spiritual realm. This implies that your spiritual nature holds deeper truths about who you are, your purpose, and your connection to something greater than yourself. *You are more!*

3. I believe the body is the temporal nature, a physical vessel that houses your eternal spiritual essence of who you truly are. *You are more!*

4. Transcendence of death. This implies that your spiritual nature continues beyond the lifespan of your physical body. It suggests the possibility of an afterlife or a continued existence in the spiritual realm, where the limitation of the physical body no longer constrains your spiritual essence. *You are more!*

ABOUT THE AUTHOR

Jocelyn Nolan Lee is a writer, educator, and entrepreneur. With a career spanning over 30 years in the financial services sector, she's a seasoned expert in business development and product marketing. Her leadership has been instrumental in fostering growth and innovation, especially within community banks and FINTECH companies.

In 2004, Jocelyn earned a fellowship with the National African American Women's Leadership Institute (NAAWLI), a non-profit organization committed to the professional development and advancement of Black women.

She's served her community on local boards in Wisconsin, spearheading financial literacy programs with Milwaukee Public Schools and the YWCA, and frequently speaking at workshops and seminars on topics ranging from religion to leadership and personal development.

Her 2014 dissertation, "Mentoring and African American Women's Advancement to Leadership Positions in Corporate America," delves into the lived experiences of African American women, exploring the impact of mentorship on their career trajectories.

Since stepping away from corporate America, Jocelyn has channeled her energies into writing, blogging about personal growth, and exploring other creative outlets. As an adjunct professor and mentor, she's passionate about uplifting others.

Jocelyn holds a BSM and MA in Religious Studies from Cardinal Stritch University, an MA in Education from Grand Canyon University, and a Doctor of Management in Organizational Leadership from the University of Phoenix.

On the personal front, Jocelyn treasures her 42-year marriage to her childhood love, Myron Lee. They are proud parents to three adult children and grandparents to four. Currently based in Arizona, Jocelyn enjoys the company of her octogenarian mother and her faithful Labrador retriever as she continues her journey of lifelong learning and growth.